MW01231468

THE *Gift,*

UNVEILED

*Introspective Devotionals on **God's** Presence*

Suzanne L. Williams

Thank you for allowing me
to share my journey + testimony
with you!   1 Thess 5:24
Love
Suzanne

The Gift, Unveiled: Introspective Devotionals on God's Presence

The author has altered several names in this book to protect the privacy of certain individuals.

Unless otherwise indicated, all scripture references are taken from NSAB (New American Standard Bible, 2020 The Lockman Foundation).

Cover image and graphics provided by artist: Mikail Wright of The Jackson Family Art Show www.familyartshow.com

Coloring pages inspired by Helen Bryant's flower photographs @ bstar360

Photographs provided by: Jasmine Williams of The Jackson Family Art Show www.familyartshow.com

www.giftunveiled.com

ISBN-13: 978-1-7361929-1-7

Acknowledgments

God, thank You for preparing and challenging me to share my testimony.

If it wasn't for God bringing these people into my journey, I am not sure this project would be complete. I want to specifically mention:

Charles and Diane Williams, Mikail and Kyle Wright, thank you for being loyal and loving.

Dorothy Johnson, Jacqueline Williams-Harlan, Billie Watts, Brenda Fortune, Sylvia Davis, thank you for loving me, unconditionally. Your recipes, good advice, and good food have sustained me in so many ways.

Joy Young, Alisa Sheard, Helen Bryant, Nealynn Waithe, thank you for more than twenty-five years of true friendship.

Bible Study Bunch: Diane, Lynn, Jasmine, Charmyonne, Jayla, Joyce, Margaret, thank you for studying the Bible and breaking bread with me, while being my test subjects.

Prayer Warrior Friends: Dawn, Dottie, Kym, Linda, Tonya, Valerie, thank you for consistently taking time to minister to your sisters and others. Thank you for praying for and with me.

Merita Jones, thank you for taking the early-morning shift with God and faithfully sending out morning devotional texts that have blessed me as well as many others.

Medley Management and Prose, Inc.—Yvonne Medley, *Red Ink Editing*—Shanice Stewart, and Reginald and Quiana Kee, thank you for helping me to translate my midnight transcriptions into a manuscript, and a manuscript into a published work of which I am proud.

You, I thank you for allowing me to share my testimony with you, and inviting me into your journey.

Contents

Section: Three

Part One

Preface

In December 2018, after watching a movie recounting a journalist's journey from atheism to preaching in a pulpit, I was awakened and told to, "prepare your testimony." Well, here it is! Some would have you to believe that He only speaks to the religiously zealous. I am a living witness to the Truth! God speaks to those living righteously and to those who are not. Please see *Week 3 God Still Speaks—On Trial.* We overcome by the blood of the Lamb and the word of our testimony.

God is right in the middle of your everyday situations, not just the huge snapshots of life. This book is my testimony—a collection of devotionals, illustrating the many ways I hear from God. I am inviting you to also acknowledge His presence in your experiences.

But please don't just take my word for it, check out the Word for yourself. Take note of who Jesus speaks to and the messages given to the varying audiences. God's Spirit is poured out on the just and the unjust—just like the rain. Thanks be to God, He is the Author and Finisher of faith, not just for this author but for you, too. Through Jesus' sacrifice and the indwelling Holy Spirit, "It is finished!" He placed everything in divine order for His plan to be complete in the fullness of time.

It's time for you to know the Truth, and to let Him set you free! Once you are free, I challenge you to use your key to reach back and set others free, too. That is what I am doing with my gift, from God, through me, to you!

I trust and pray this book has made its way to you at the perfect time, and will leave you forever changed!

Suzanne L. Williams | i

Introduction — God speaks!

I heard whispers, "You're a warrior," and "Dunamis." These were some of the first I remember.

Dunamis? I thought. I had never heard of the word. He spoke to me on a September morning in 2010, and that same day in my office breakroom, a co-worker invited me to a conference at his church.

"The theme is Dunamis," he said to me.

I was a little startled, but I wanted to know more. I googled it and found this: *It means that this person … has some inner strength that does not depend on outward things.*

The first time I realized how much He does speak, and how clearly, He responded poetically to a poem I had written. I was asking God why things had to be the way they were in my life. In my poem, titled *If I Can Say What I Want to Say*, I released what I felt: frustrated, confused, doubtful, worried, disappointed, scared, tired, and lonely.

In a fitting response, God gave me:

If I Could Listen to What is Being Said

The Creator works most creatively,

He will work it out Suzie, wait and see.

His plan, His design, His creation, His view,

Aspirations, promises, are all for you.

He created you for a purpose

never forget, forfeit, give up.

Stand strong in your faith,

and it won't take long.

Why do you let others see what you can't see?

Why present something, and long to be viewed differently?

Why never give a chance, and long to be desired,

admired, treasured, when your look says, "You're fired!"

Why give part, and want the whole?

Why give sex, when you want the soul?

It don't take a whole day to recognize sunshine, it's true.

But with a frown, mask, hater-blockers, moods, winter down coat, and sun blocking curtains,

you expect them to see the real you?

I put you on a hill for everyone to see,

Not just who you are, but also see Me.

But you are afraid, disdain, and oh so shy.

When people want to talk, you want to know why.

When a connection is desired, you say,

"Naw, not today!

No vacancy, no postings, on vacation, please go away!

I'm out to lunch and won't be back again,

I don't need you for a confidant, lover, or friend!

I'm good! Now please go away!"

But in the back of your mind,

you want them to stay.

You want them to take the time to see,

not only you, but also Me.

The good I Am, the changes I've made,

 Maybe they coulda if they woulda stayed...

"I never thought you'd leave in autumn,

You said you'd be there when it rained,

Why didn't you stay?"

Is what you cry, beg, and plead,

"Why can't they be psychic and discern my need?"

I Am the God that supplies all of your need.

I put it in at creation, it is just a seed.

Water it, nourish it, give it room to grow.

But if you don't, you will never know,

Your purpose, your dream, passions, desires, your fuel.

What you can provide to a world so cruel.

Not an accident, not a happenstance, circumstance, or a situation,

I brought you here to change a nation!

Change a face, change a heart, change a mind, reconnect.

I got you baby, no need to fret.

That was just basic training.

Now you're ready to

March

April

May

As long as you stay,

In the Word, on your grind,

Free your soul, free your mind.

Enjoy your gifts.

Marvel at your talents.

Stay connected, be in balance.

Not only mother of the Brothers Wright,

Not the mother of flight,

Mother of the Good Fight!

Suzanne L. Williams | v

I told you, you're a warrior.

Are you willing?

In that gap, will you be the filling?

You're on candid camera, live candidly!

Let the world enjoy what I've created you to be!

***

I replied, crying:

Thank You, Father!

I know You truly love me,

I'll face the world with more certainty!

To this day, reading this poem shakes me, moves me, motivates me, makes me cry, and awes me!

What we hear is not always easy to accept, obey, or share. Sometimes we may not even understand what is being said. At times I've even considered it a burden. But now I see it as a gift, and I would like to share it with you. More so, God wants to share His gift with you.

New Year's morning, 2016, in my secret place, I hear, "I want you to write a book."

My quick response was, "You know I don't like to write."

His quicker response, "I know," was accompanied with a download of titles and topics. They came so quickly, I struggled to type them all. I don't think I've seen my thumbs move so fast.

When I walked out of my bathroom, apparently one of our more popular places to meet, I had a list of more than forty topics. I am not sure how many actually ended up in this book, but it helped me to understand that in my weakness, He is truly strong. This is only a small portion of what He has given me over the past few years.

His ability to speak supersedes my perceived disabilities. His favorite time to speak seems to be in the middle of the night. I've been told that is one of the times when I'm quiet enough to hear. I am thankful to God for aligning me with Kingdom workers, helping to translate some of my midnight transcriptions.

What I Hope you
Receive from this Journey

My prayer, and desire, is for your spiritual senses to be opened and attuned, allowing you to perceive and acknowledge God in all His ways, no matter when or how He chooses. He is speaking to you. I am sharing my experiences to show you how God has gone outside of my small box of religion to demonstrate His Love toward me—and you, too.

These devotionals have been used in the Bible Studies of my friends and family, co-hosted with my one of my closest friends, Lynn. We have spent many evenings eating, fellowshipping, reading multiple Bible translations, discussing, debating, laughing, praying—just sharing and growing closer to each other and to God.

You can use the notes pages after each devotional as a tool to start writing what He is revealing to you. You can capture your prayers, verses, poems, songs, questions, challenge responses, or anything that comes to your mind, spirit, and soul. Just start writing!

Are you ready for this journey in your full armor?

"Stand firm therefore, by fastening the belt of truth around your waist, by putting on the breastplate of righteousness, by fitting your feet with the preparation that comes from the good news of peace, and in all of this, by taking up the shield of faith with which you can extinguish all the flaming arrows of the evil one. And take the helmet of salvation and the sword of the Spirit, which is the Word of God." (Ephesians 6:14-17, New English Translation)

Don't Forget Your Sword!

The Gift, Unveiled should not be considered a substitute for the Bible in any way, shape or form. It is important to be intimate with your own Bible, it's your Sword! At the end of each devotional, I added a list of scriptures. The verses listed are not the only appropriate verses for these devotionals. I wanted to provide at least one verse or passage for daily meditation. But I challenge you to read the full chapter for a full understanding. It is important to allow the Holy Spirit to guide you. I do this by saying a prayer, asking for things pertinent to my walk to be illuminated by Him. God may show you additional scriptures and learning tools to consider.

If I tell my son to take out the trash and he doesn't do it, but then later when someone else tells him, if he says, "Oh that's confirmation, my mom told me to take out the trash, let me go do it," I may punish him! He needs to move when I speak because I am the authority. I have his best interest in mind and we both know that doesn't need confirmation. Sometimes it is taught that we should seek confirmation after God has spoken to us. I don't believe that. I am His sheep and I know His voice. When He says move, I move in faith, and sometimes I get confirmation along the way through other messages, advice, songs, etc. That said, I know He is sovereignly my authority.

Luke 17:11-14 NASB says, "While He was on the way to Jerusalem, He was passing between Samaria and Galilee. As He entered a village, ten leprous men who stood at a distance met Him; and they raised their voices, saying, 'Jesus, Master, have mercy on us!' When He saw them, He said to them, 'Go and show yourselves to the priests.' And as they were going, they were cleansed."

What if they would have waited for confirmation after hearing from God, I wonder if they would have been healed? I can't afford to wait for man to confirm for me what I hear directly from My Father! While I can't tell anyone how he or she will or should hear the voice of God, this book illustrates the many ways I hear from God.

While studying, I find it interesting to read some commonly-known scriptures in multiple translations. Some seem to speak the message in different ways. For example, later in one of the devotionals, *Week 39— America, the Glutton*, you'll find:

"But this kind does not go out except by prayer and fasting." (Matthew 17:21, NASB)

However, this is not the way it reads in certain translations of the Bible. An online Bible source can help you study several translations at once.

Let's open in prayer and then, unveil this gift.

God, I thank You for opening Yourself to me and then opening me to others. Open eyes, hearts, and minds to You, Lord God. Allow us to see You, ourselves, and others in the way You do. Allow us to exchange our small thoughts and preconceived ideas for the Truth. Shift paradigms, break strongholds, and cleanse and purify us of old mindsets in the Mighty Name of Jesus! Thank You for Your goodness, grace, and mercy! Thank You for speaking my language! Thank You for the Translator, Comforter, and Guide! You are truly my everything, and I am grateful.

Now unto Him, who is able to do exceedingly and abundantly above all that I can ask, think or think to ask, be all honor, glory, dominion, and power forever. Amen!

With love and adoration,

Your girl,

Suzanne

Dedicated to Gladys B. Wells, She Was a Very Special Lady — My Grandma Kept It 100

I wanted to finish this book to celebrate my family matriarch. Throughout her life, she fought the good fight and I believe she is peacefully resting. However, I wasn't finished with *The Gift, Unveiled*, and clearly the book was not finished with me by my self-imposed November 1, 2019 deadline either.

Shaking up the Roots

For my grandma's 100th birthday my oldest son, my mom and I commemorated the day by repotting four houseplants. These were originally my grandmother's plants and have been in my family for more than fifty years. My mom ensured I had a clipping from two of the plants when I moved into my own house. The plants draw the attention of all who visit my home. I didn't realize two small vines could multiply so much. They cascade over the banister and greet visitors at the door. I think it helps them to arrive and depart in peace.

One of the plants is a Coleus. One visitor commented that he was surprised to see this plant, that he was so familiar with seeing in Florida, inside a house in Maryland. He mentioned that they grow outdoors everywhere in the town where he grew up. He also told me that the roots were often used to make a tea to heal heart ailments. I knew my grandma was into natural remedies, like myself, but it made my heart warm to know that there could be healing found in the roots of the plants she passed on from generation to generation.

Several months ago, I noticed the plants at my mom's house weren't thriving as much as the ones at my house. The plants were all reproducing and starting to cover her window, but I noticed the leaves were a lot larger on the plants at my house. I offered to come and repot the plants with her. It was taking me a long while to get around to fulfilling my offer, but I knew I wanted to do something to celebrate my grandmother's 100th birthday with my mom. Finally, my mother reminded me of my offer, and we got right to repotting the plants.

Each plant had to be untangled and pruned. We had to loosen the old nutrient-deficient soil from these root-bound plants. Afterward we added some fresh organic soil and replaced the manicured plants back in their pots. We thought we would have to buy bigger pots but realized once we shook off the old dirt there was plenty of space for new soil.

The plants looked happy when we placed them back on the window seal. I was happy that I could see out of the unobstructed bay window again. My mom was so happy, she put on a shirt that she had given my grandma nearly twenty years prior. As a Christmas present my mom got a shirt made with a picture of my grandma holding her first two great-grandchildren, my cousin's daughter, Emoni, and my oldest son, Mikail. Mikail gave my mom a mini photo shoot with the plants. My mom smiled that same big smile that I remember my grandma had. I think she passed it on to me, too.

That night, during prayer, my oldest son thanked God for shaking up the roots. I pray that we allow Him to shake whatever needs to be shaken. So, we aren't so entangled in the old that we don't partner with Him as He does a new thing.

Her Legacy

I remember my grandma seemed to always have a cake in her kitchen that she had made for someone, from scratch of course, and a small one-layered taster cake waiting for us. She allowed us to taste and see that what she was cooking up was good! My favorite was and, thanks to the passed-on recipe and training, still is a three-layer chocolate cake. That is what we call it. It's really a white cake with chocolate frosting, but the chocolate is what makes this cake what it is.

She was the strongest warrior I knew. I am certain that her prayers availed much in my life. Her health battles later in her life, showed a long-suffering and patient endurance that I've only read about. She did not complain. It was obvious that she believed and did what she was taught in church, and what she read in her Bible. Nothing stopped her from praying, praising, singing, worshiping, and helping others with a genuine smile on her melanin-rich, wrinkle-free face. She stayed with my parents often when she was sick and healing. But as soon as she got better, she was moving around the top floor of their house in a wheelchair to see where she could be helpful. And she did it. Even after she became a double amputee, I would find her in my parents' room making their beds while they were at work.

Her prayers, plants, recipes, big smile, and mandate that her household was going to serve the Lord, left an indelible fingerprint on the family. We are far from perfect, but she ensured we were connected to the True Vine. I will produce a good harvest and develop other disciples as a *Thank You* to God and my grandma.

As with all of us, she seemed to share a special bond with my oldest son, Mikail. Although she was disappointed when he missed being born on her birthday by a few days, they seemed liked old friends. He was just a couple of weeks old when their friendship was made evident to me. They would spend hours just talking. I thought newborns were supposed to be quiet. But I could hear them contently having deep conversations for hours until his babbling would stop because he fell asleep, or needed food, or a change.

Stir up the gift

The weekend of my Grandmother's 100th birthday celebration, we also got together as a family to celebrate Mikail's twenty-first birthday. We ate the same chocolate cake that my grandma always said she hoped was, "okay." It was always great! Growing up, my mom used to come home early from Trick-or-Treating to ensure she made a cake for my grandma's birthday. Now she makes the cake for all of us but is looking for someone who will be willing to learn the craft. I would offer, but I am still not the best in following institutions and recipes to the letter. The Lord is still working on me.

He filled me with the oil of gladness when He introduced me to Gladys. She was a very special lady, and although it has been more than fifteen years, I still miss you granny. She is a very special lady to me.

Verses:

Psalm 45:6

Hebrews 1:9

Isaiah 61:3

Proverbs 13:22

Ecclesiastes 2:21

2 Timothy 1:6

Proverbs 12:3

Challenge:

Think about what legacies have been passed down in your family. Are you passing down the same things for future generations? What would you like to be a part of your legacy?

Prayer:

Thank You God for the generational legacies and blessings in my family. May we know that we have been blessed in order to be a blessing to others. Amen!

My Notes

WEEK 2

My Testimony

One December evening in 2018, after watching a movie detailing a journalist's journey from atheism to preaching in a pulpit, God told me to prepare my testimony. This has been the most difficult devotional to write. It didn't pour out of me like many of the others did. After many months of God reminding me about my testimony, I struggled. My few inspired spurts only led up to seemingly disconnected mash-ups. However, as with all the other devotionals, there is a connection.-

How do you distill a whole lifetime to explain who you are to someone who doesn't know you? What highlights do you remember and share?

I was about to dive in at the beginning, then she stopped me.

"Where did the kids come from?" My editor asked.

The Kids

I met RW through a friend when we were both fourteen. We used to spend hours and hours talking on the phone. A lot of times we would either fall asleep on the phone or watch the sunrise together. When I was old enough to drive, I would borrow or steal my parents' car to spend those hours with him, in person, when possible. We had an on-again-off-again relationship. Sometimes breaking up for a year before getting back together. A big breakup came when I went off to college, about an hour away. But I still called him all the time and told him I loved him, while I dated someone with the same initials and a similar birthday.

Sometime before my sophomore year, we decided to make our relationship work. I would either come home from Baltimore on the weekends or he would come up and spend the weekends with me. The love songs of mid-'90s R&B supplied the soundtrack to my life. The albums: *Baduism, Who is Jill Scott, Velvet Rope,* and *Love Jones* were in constant rotation. In 1998, we were nineteen years old and Valentine's Day fell on a Saturday. And we made it a whole weekend affair. A few weeks later, I found out that we had created our *love child,* as we would call him for several years.

We discussed marriage before and after we got the news. We even had a date planned. The day of fall equinox 2000, we planned to make the pledge of forever. It seemed inevitable; we had always found our way back to one another in the past. But that was before love changed. I didn't love him, unconditionally. I wonder, now, if I loved him at all, or if he was just familiar, nice to me, and willing to tell me he loved me.

After I had our son, I decided I wanted to go back to school and be close to campus. We found an apartment together and lived there for about a year. Instead of getting married, we pretended that we were. Our home was filled with game nights, good food, potty training, low funds, small paychecks, bills, a few arguments, and fun.

We struggled with a lot during our relationship, but the struggle with addiction really ended it for us. His was with substances, and mine was with control. I knew what was right and how everyone could live a good life, regardless of how I was living mine. I was never shy about sharing my unsolicited views. By the time our son was five, we had broken up many times, but I decided this was the last time. I had to question myself, was I just with him because I had been with him so long and had invested so much?

"Y'all broke up? So, where did the second baby come from?" my inquisitive editor wanted to know.

After another, I guess I can call it a breakup—although we never were officially together— I was searching for comfort. RW was familiar, and we already had to see each other on occasion because of our son. I found comfort in him. It only took a few weekend visits for me to discover I was pregnant. I knew it right away. It was definitely not immaculate conception, more like immaculate contraception. We just weren't careful at all. Perhaps being comfortable also meant I was not careful.

I actually really wanted the baby, and I was hopeful that things would work out—although nothing had changed. But it quickly became evident that it wasn't going to work. I figured that if I could have a baby at twenty years old, and do a decent job of rearing him, then surely at twenty-seven, I could do a good job rearing number two. At the time, I was working and had gone back to school—after stopping and starting several times—and I took care of my oldest son. I had my parents' constant support, even though I know they wanted better for my life. They helped me make it work. Their love for me was truly unconditional. Maybe I kept returning to RW thinking we would share the same type of unconditional love that my parents shared. My parents meant forever when they made their vows. They worked hard, because they figured out early in their relationship that it actually took work—things don't just work out on their own.

We never got back together. And even to this day, we can still barely have a conversation without someone arguing, yelling, or hanging up. "But I am glad, you asked the question," I said to my newfound friend and dutiful inquisitor. It gave me the chance to remember that we didn't always disagree. We actually did like one another, and that is where our two well-earned children came from. I love you Mikail and Kyle!

This journey led me closer to my—and my sons'—Heavenly Father. It also gave me a better understanding and clearer view of my loving parents.

Verses:

1 John 1:9-10

Job 15:11-14

Psalm 127: 3-4

Matthew 18:10

Mark 10:16

Proverbs 22:15

Ephesians 6:1-4

Challenge:

Think about a challenging time in your life. Go back and write any good details that you can identify, and the lessons learned. God uses our challenging seasons to mature and bless us.

Prayer:

God, I thank You for always including some good in the story. You are good, even when we, or circumstances, are not. Please help us to renew our mind and remember the benefits of all the challenges You have seen us through.

Thank You for never leaving nor forsaking me. Thank You for giving me good and loving parents. Thank You for being the perfect Father for my sons and me! I love You. Amen!

My Notes

WEEK 3

God Still Speaks — On Trial

I swear that the evidence I shall give in this matter is the truth, the whole truth and nothing but the truth, so help me God!

For the record, my name is Suzanne. It means Lily. I have been told that I am a lily but not just of the valley. My family calls me Suzie. Apparently, I've had this nickname since before I was born. When my mom was carrying me, she kept telling me, "Suzie, stop kicking me!" This is a much better name choice than what my older sister would have picked, if she had been able. Shani told the whole family that she had a name for the new baby, Amazing Johnson! I was born to Charles—meaning free man, and Diane— meaning complete light, divine, heavenly. I am their middle daughter—like the best part of a cookie or a sandwich!

Prosecution:

God speaks, okay! But why would God speak to you?

What theology school did you graduate from?

None, I see, well what church do you attend?

At a very young age, I attended a Baptist church. I was about ten or eleven when I decided to get baptized. I know a foundation was laid there which sustained me throughout the ignorance of my adolescence. My family left that church when I was about twelve.

I didn't go back to church, on a regular basis, until I was in my early twenties. My oldest son was about three, and he asked me to come to church with him and my family. So I attended my family's non-denominational church for a few years and I really enjoyed being in church with four generations of us worshipping in a church where my cousin was the pastor. I was surrounded by my family, weekly. But then I stopped attending again after my grandmother passed. I stayed away for several more years until after my second son was born. One day, at a local store, I ran into another cousin from the church, he simply stated that he missed me being there. I went back that next Sunday, and then was a regular, again, for about seven more years. I taught in children's church, and attended Sunday Services and Bible Studies, regularly, until I got the Word to leave. This scripture was given to me for my journey.

"The Lord said to Abram: Leave your country, your family, and your relatives and go to the land that I will show you." (Genesis 12:1, CEV)

After a couple of months of visiting local churches, my sons and I found, and agreed upon, another church-home that felt like family. I spent more than seven years fellowshipping, worshipping, serving, leading children's church, and ministering there. I got another prophetic message, and other words, confirming what I felt; it was time to leave. I tried to find a substitute. I went to several churches, but then received a message to stop that search and spend time with just Him.

Prosecution:

This is unbelievable, Your Honor!

No degree!

No church-home!

No covering!

Right now, I am homeschooled. I think it is just for a season. The first week was very freeing, I had more time on my hands, but I was struggling with how to use this freedom for the Kingdom. From what was shared with me, I knew I wasn't supposed to watch a sermon or message online. So, I was going to watch one of the Gospels of Matthew, Mark, Luke, or John movies. But I heard Him say, "watch whatever you want, I can speak to you through anything." So, I decided on a movie of which its title caught my attention a few days before. Not too long after the movie started, a page of the Bible flashed on the screen. I had to rewind and pause the movie to see what it was; the page was Proverbs 3. The passage Proverbs 3:5-6 has been showing up in my life, notably, for at least the past five years. This scene and several others in the movie reminded me that God can and will use whatever He deems necessary to speak to His beloved children.

In the meantime, I do occasionally, as led, attend church services, prayers, outreach programs, and home fellowships. I am continuing with the other personal things that I have done for a long time, now, which is to spend solitary time with God to learn more about Him and what He wants from me. And at times, I have heard the Voice of God. The first message I remember receiving was that I was a warrior. He speaks to me by leading me to passages in The Word. He also speaks to me through the words of others, my children, and even by way of my own advice given to others. I receive His messages in books, movies, nature, my dreams—and when I am quiet enough to hear it directly, in a still small voice.

Prosecution:

Homeschool?! Come on jury, did you hear that? We all know the kids who are homeschooled don't learn anything, aren't ready for the real world, and they are too sheltered.

My oldest son was drowning when I pulled him out of our public school system. With the education I received, I had high, but unmet, expectations. I decided to homeschool him. He went from close to failing his freshman year to graduating from high school a year early. He started college at sixteen and has studied and traveled internationally. I also homeschooled my younger son for several years before he transitioned back to public school for the eighth grade. Knowing that education is available outside of the public system, when God called me to come out of my previous church I had to go #TeamHomeschool!

I Was Educated like the Talented Tenth

I tested, got selected in the lottery and apparently, received a golden ticket. It was front page news, not just in my family or with friends and loved ones, I was also in *The Washington Post!* I was part of the first class in the TAG magnet program in the Prince George's County Public School System. They separated and trained us to see the world differently, think critically, and effect change. I didn't know about limitations; I knew I could be anything I wanted when I grew up. I know pastors, doctors, lawyers, business owners, entrepreneurs, politicians and authors who were groomed in this and similar programs across the nation.

In the '80s, I went to a school that was equipped with an Apple computer lab as well as a PC computer lab. They even provided us with a computer for home. I went on numerous field trips each year and completed my science fair project, yearly, with fond memories. I even wrote and self-published several write-a-books.

They groomed us to see ourselves as part of the whole, with micro and macro place projects as an example. These group projects helped us to understand our role within family and the community. In my multi-ethnic classes, I really didn't know racism, sexism, or classism existed. This gave me a skewed view, and I thought everyone was being afforded the same opportunities. I didn't understand that those who lived in the same single-family home neighborhood with me, on tree-lined streets, attended schools that lacked any of the extravagances that I only knew as normal. I certainly didn't know that children who looked like me were experiencing many more serious injustices in my country. Of course, I didn't consider the atrocities suffered by melanin-rich people across the world.

The training worked. Nobody told me girls didn't like math or science. I was a math and computer science major in high school. I took advanced placement and international baccalaureate classes. I excelled in calculus, chemistry, and computer classes in my high school. I was trained to write computer programs and had preliminary knowledge that would allow me to code something that didn't even exist yet—the public-accessed Internet. I graduated with a university high school distinguished diploma. I was recognized in *The Who's Who* among high school senior's publication. I was accepted into the University of Maryland, Baltimore County (UMBC), an honors university in my state. #RetrieverPride! I was groomed well and am currently successful in the IT field. My empathy, that has caused me to feel the pain of others, pushed me into the usability specialty within the field. The focus is on people and what they need as a requirement.

To Whom Much is Given, Much is Required

These worldly accomplishments, I've described, mean nothing in the lens of eternity. It wouldn't profit me anything to gain the whole world but lose my soul in the process. My soul was definitely hanging in the balance. I was not doing anything for the Kingdom or to give honor, glory or dominion to the only wise God Our Father. I was self-centered and I wasn't bearing any fruit of the Spirit. I was blind, habitually sinning with little-to-no remorse. God was gracious enough to show me, through several of my dreams, that this type of sin leads to death.

Around 3 a.m. on my birthday in 2019, I was inspired to write again. His gift to me is allowing me to correct not only how I see Him, but also how I see and value myself. I'm sure you will pick up on it: I can be flawed, unaware, strong, stubborn, obedient, loving, sarcastic, giving, and so many other characteristics. I was given a message that comfort has been my idol. Leaving that behind, I am now willing to allow His hand and Spirit to recycle and shape me to be His vessel; to be used as He wills. He is always in the process of perfecting us, anyway. Then He clues me in on the process by making the request for me to do something, that my limited mindset convinced me was impossible, while assuring me that I have already been performing that deed successfully through Him.

I had the opportunity to sit with two sets of six ladies that week. What they chose to share was eye opening in retrospect and finally allowed me to complete this devotional. I sat and talked with ladies whom I met through church. What they shared was interesting, and it wasn't the self-righteous, make-me-look-good, feel-good testimony that one might expect. We revealed initial impressions and how our experiences proved to be similar or different from the preconceptions of life. They were raw, funny, and honest!

I then sat with a group of women writers of color.

They posed a question, "What does freedom mean to you?"

My answer was, "Freedom meant I have my own voice and perspective without having to silence or convince someone else that they are wrong. It's okay for it to be uniquely mine without me having to explain, justify, or apologize for it."

Again, with fresh eyes, I realize that we all carefully decide what we choose to share. Depending on the audience and how similar or dissimilar they are to what you are motivated to portray at that time tells a lot. Unconsciously, these episodes have been curated to share in this book. They are not only the highlights, but also, some of these I would mark for the bloopers reel. They show me in the journey, not at the end.

I most likely don't know you at all and have no idea what will help you to feel I am qualified to speak on these topics. I lack many of the titles and holy experiences that draw the religious crowd. I've had rank, tenure, years and regularity of church attendance, and titles pulled on me numerous times during my journey. I feel it was those things that justified others in their attempt to spruce up and fictionalize my life's story to fit inside their mindset box.

Prosecution:

My black sister,

Have you heard about a slave ship named, Jesus?

Christianity is a white man's religion!

There wasn't even a 'J' in those times, so how could His name be Jesus?

That pastor just wants people's money!

Do you know even the Bible was used to enforce slavery?!

I have a video that once you see it, you will renounce your faith!

I'm a witness, God has always been there for me, blessing me in ways that I can't even begin to understand; I'm not *that* smart! Proverbs 3:5-6 follows me to admonish and remind me to not lean on my world-given identity as *smart*, but to trust Him! He is constantly preparing me for His desired end.

Just like I'm not able to understand, explain, or unwrite the content of these devotionals and the countless other chapters of my life, I don't have the answers for all the questions or accusations that I encounter as a Christian. I am only prepared to give an answer for why I have faith. This week's devotional, and this entire collection of devotionals, is my testimony of the gift that God has given to me, outside the box. These stories illustrate many parts of my life but are only a snapshot into my previously unwritten diary.

I'm hopeful that through my sharing, you will benefit from what is written. I'm hopeful it encourages you to examine and become more familiar with your armor and sword. I pray this book pushes you closest to God—allowing Him to reveal the real *you* to you, from His perspective. So, He can change you into the very image of Christ, by using your gifts, talents, and deficiencies to fulfill your specific purpose and position in the Body.

My experience is unapologetically mine and correct from my perspective. My goal is not to change you into me, but to help us gain a greater appreciation for how special the Creative Creator created us all to be. These perspectives add depth to our perception of the Almighty. What if instead of placing so much emphasis on being right or wrong about fellowship or religion, one's emphasis or concern would have much more to do with a God-inspired vantage point. That should be acknowledged and valued above all, as He is weaving together nature and nurture, experience and environments, good and evil for our good.

God is good and His mercy endures forever! So, now my perception has changed. I now see I have been blessed to be a blessing to others. I'm flawed, but willing. Humbled by the experiences shared in this book and so many more. I have become continuously, no matter where I am, open and sensitive to the Holy Spirit. Grateful to be justified and considered worthy by the Most High God, through the Blood of the Lamb. Ready and equipped by the words of this testimony for whatever comes next!

In the beginning, the Spirit of God moved and quickened me. He spoke a Word, it was crafted and shaped until I revealed who I am, to hopefully help you see who you are. On this note, I'm hopeful the Prosecution rests!

Prosecution:

I think she just needs to be quiet or get locked up for contempt. She seems like a false witness!

God:

I've heard enough. She is my credible witness. Case dismissed!

Verses:

*Proverbs 3:5-6

**Ecclesiastes 9:11

**Matthew 5:45

***Romans 5:10

****John 8:26

****Revelation 12:11

**** Galatians 1:11-12

*This passage follows me, just like Grace and Mercy. I see it quite regularly!

**given to me in a dream to deliver to someone

*** verse of the day on Biblegateway.com

**** the small voice reminded me of these

Challenge:

Write your testimony. Pay special attention to what you have shared and what you chose not to share. Ask God to reveal what your words and omissions have spoken about the condition of your heart. Also, ask Him to illuminate the Word to supply you with scriptural evidence that supports your testimony.

Prayer:

Thank You, God for the revelation of my gift. Now that it is unveiled, I will not hide it. I am sharing it with the world. I love You! Amen!

My Notes

WEEK 4

The Final Exam –
Shaken Not Stirred

I woke up and my house was shaking! I heard something, it sounded huge, much larger than what I usually hear coming into the Joint Base Andrews-Naval Air Facility that I live near. I was scared. *God please protect me, my friends, family and loved ones*, was part of my silent prayer as I drifted back to sleep. But then I woke back up. I had fallen asleep while letting the BibleGateway App read me the chapter from the Verse of the Day, and then apparently many more chapters for hours after that. When I was about to turn that off, I saw I had missed several texts. My older sister sent one at 5:11 a.m., it just said, "Okay" in reply to a group text. Then I saw ten more. *What, why so early?* I wondered. One of the sisters with whom I used to attend church had sent an urgent prayer request group text. Everyone was awake and on it. Sending prayers and texts, immediately. Most of these texts came in at 5:11 a.m.

Within this group, we have experienced nearly everything together: life, death, good, bad, and indifferent. Over the previous year, we had spent time ministering not only to our sisters in this group, but also, we started to minister to others. Once a month, we visited a local nursing home and rehabilitation center. We read, played games, prayed, and brought snacks and other tokens of love. We also got together afterward to eat and just enjoy one another other.

It felt very unfortunate when I had to write these words a year before, when I found out about the death of my friend's son. But I felt fortunate to have the scriptures for this situation. I shared with the ladies, *Week 51—The Warrior's Arsenal*. That contains the Word for such a time as this tragic one. I also shared a text.

"Praying and I sent an email. All I hear is, "it's go-time!" I feel I am being tested on everything I claim to know about God. We have to be ready. I'm never up this early, but a loud something just landed at Andrews Air Force Base shaking me out of my sleep. I was actually scared. Then I saw a text from my sister, and y'all sisters. I love y'all. Please armor up!"

I also realized I still had not committed those verses to my memory. I have to get on it! Then I had to look up number five hundred eleven (511) in the *Strong's Concordance*. Hebrew Elqanah: "God has created," or "God has taken possession," the name of several Israelites. Greek Anóteros: "higher to a more honorable place (at the dinner table); previously, in an earlier passage (or a book), above."

We memorize and quote Psalm 23, religiously. How can we believe *He prepares a table before me in the presence of my enemies*, but also find it unbelievable that we have enemies, haters, and bad situations? If He is leading us through the valley where the shadow of death is, we must follow. It may be where we finally die to self. Or maybe He will have us there to speak to the dry bones. We have to go if we want to find out and see Him do the miraculous.

A couple of weeks prior, I received shocking news in the family. It shook my faith, but I couldn't lose faith. It uncovered dirt and unhealed toxic family roots. We had generational curses that nobody wanted to face. It seems we all thought praying while watching was enough, but we were wrong. I was busy putting final touches on this manuscript. Then time ran out. Boom! All the pieces flew, I felt like some of them and a piece of me also got blown up—completely destroyed.

I was carefully playing *Perfection*, trying my best to do the right thing, say the right thing, write the right thing, believe the right thing. So, God had to make sure nothing bad would ever happen to me, my family, friends or loved ones, right?! Wrong! That is a lie that needs to go back to the pits of Hell from which it came. It's sadly taught across the pulpit, too. *Pay your tithes, God will protect your stuff.* Like He is the eternal good neighbor. God is much better than an insurance policy, ensuring that we make it to Heaven, someday. He gave it all for us to bring Heaven to Earth and set captives free, now.

As I was reeling, and healing, I didn't hear God speak to me very much. I got out the things I felt by talking, praying, crying, journaling.

My honest and raw notes, during this time, captured how I felt:

» Lost

» Overwhelmed

» Tired

» Confused

» Hurt

- » Sad

- » Torn

- » Like a failure as mom

- » Like my discernment is off

- » Like I don't know the next step or any of the path

- » Broken

- » Like the formula didn't work, it didn't stop us from getting hurt or hurting others

- » Like I don't want to finish this book

- » Alone

- » Partially blind

- » Like I still have to show up

- » Like I'm supposed to know what to do without being helped

- » I want to get away

- » Most of the time it seems like a waste of time to ask for help. It takes time to ask, explain, beg, wait, be disappointed, have to find out what was done, clean it up, and then fix it. Why?

- » Not fair

- » I have enough on my plate, nothing is ever removed just more piled on

- » Like everyone's dump

- » Like the emergency room

- » Unseen

- » Forgotten

» On call 24/7 mentally, physically, spiritually, emotionally

» Misunderstood: nobody knows or understands my burdens and loads

» Try not to cause waves, but that is my purpose

  » I am a generational curse breaker!

  » I am a warrior!

» Frustrated

» This is a *manure-y* situation

» I can't stay despondent. There is hope, healing

» Roots need to be healed, shaken, loosed, repotted

» It has festered for years, decades, generations

» It must stop!

» I don't want this to be my life or the theme of my life

» I don't want to feel forced to act in those pre-prescribed ways in which I see why people lose the faith!

» It is taught that if we follow the formula, we, and our family, will be protected— won't go through, but that is not the truth!

» He will never leave or forsake, that is the truth!

The only thing I heard clearly in my spirit was *if these things only happen to families in which no one is praying, believing, or connected to Me, how would healing take place?* Ugh, that made sense even to me, but this is hard. Too hard, too much to bear. I can't cling onto the false hope from a verse that doesn't exist. God does give us too much to bear on our own. The burdens and loads of our lives lead us closer to Him, and gives us a chance to minister to one another, too. While we are on our knees, in an emergency room, or a spiritual ICU, He can heal us thoroughly. No bandages just covering what is broken. God doesn't make us into a mummy. He transforms us into the very image of Himself.

I would have preferred for my gift to just be stirred up. Writing *The Gift, Unveiled* has been a tough journey. God prescribed for it to shake me to the core. Shaking off all that can be shaken.

Verses:

Hebrews 12:26-29

Psalm 23:1-6

Haggai 2: 6-9 & 21 (Read the whole chapter.)

Isaiah 13:13

Nehemiah 5:13

Isaiah 42:13

2 Timothy 1:6

Challenge:

Make a note of your challenging time and what God is revealing to you about some incorrect thoughts you had about the issue, yourself, or God. Allow Him to shake off the falsehoods and reveal the truth.

Prayer:

God, You are still good! I don't fully understand, but I love You and I trust You. You are all wise. I am not. Amen!

My Notes

Funeral Tapestry

In May 2019, I attended my cousin, Debra J. Clark's, homegoing service in Charlotte, North Carolina. This was the first funeral that part of my family had to endure since Debra's grandmother passed more than twenty-five years prior, also from cancer. The family knew that she and her brother, Howard, had battled cancer for the past few years. It seemed that almost as soon as one went into remission, the other received a diagnosis. We didn't realize how desperate her situation had become, until a couple weeks before her passing. My cousin let the family know that she was tired and had made all of her final arrangements. We were shocked and heartbroken.

On our way back home to Maryland from the funeral, we went to the Bechtler Museum. I saw my first tapestry exhibit. We admired each one and talked about how beautiful they were, and how much time it must have taken to create such large masterpieces. But what I know is that the unseen side of each tapestry is a mass of jumbled knots and frays. After I walked through the exhibit, I realized God had done it again. He had opened my eyes to another life lesson. He also comforted me at the same time.

God is the God of decency and order. Whether or not we can understand the things that God allows on this side of glory depends on our willingness to allow Him to reveal them to us. We can view His beautiful tapestry of life, once we die to self. You can choose to view it now, before your physical death or after it is all finished.

I later shared with my cousin, Jamie, that her mother's passing allowed the family to experience something beautiful. I didn't negate how difficult it still is for everyone to deal with, but I let her know how the funeral had brought the family back together. During the week of her funeral, I was able to see and spend time with many family members whom I hadn't seen in many years. The family is even closer now, we are enjoying the time that we can spend together. We are making the time and effort to show up for one another more often.

The Butterfly

I don't know struggle; I just know beauty.

It's not just what you can see,

It's a process for me.

Every hurt, every scar, beautifully woven into tapestry,

Is what beautifully makes you, you.

And has beautifully made me, me.

In the fullness of time you will clearly see,

The purpose of the process, molding what your story will be.

Every piece like a puzzle, not beautiful 'til the end.

Every pain, illness, and sorrow, in time will mend.

Nothing missing, nothing broken,

Just recast and reset.

Metamorphosis in your chrysalis,

Until your purpose is met.

Please don't damage me trying to set me free.

Struggle is the process that makes you, you.

And me like a butterfly, me.

I must go through, there is no staying here.

No holding onto what I held dear.

To stay is to die,

But when I go through, I'm a butterfly.

Soaring, inspiring, and beautifying,

All through the struggle, testifying.

Beauty beyond the surface.

Fortified with purpose.

Verses:

Romans 8:28

Ephesians 1:9

Romans 5:3-5

2 Samuel 16:12

Deuteronomy 23:5

Psalm 25:18

Psalm 73:1

Challenge:

Have an open mind for God to show you how all things are working together for your good, growth, and maturation. List several situations that seemed negative at the time and the positive impact it had on your character.

Prayer:

Thank You, God, for perfecting us. You are good and Your mercy endures forever. I love You! Amen!

My Notes

WEEK 6

Welcome to Whitmire

It's a modest town in South Carolina where my dad, his siblings, and his parents grew up. It's the kind of place where you are local news when you come into town. A place where most people stop, smile—showing teeth—and wave. A place where it's okay to just stop by without calling first. A place where you will have conversations with people you don't know, because they knew your parents growing up; and remember, they haven't seen you since you were a baby. It's a place where everyone has a nickname. You may be called something normal like *Suzie*, *Jackie* or *Dot*. If you don't know you have a nickname, it's probably because you may be referred to as *Channel 7*, *Big-belly*, *Half-head*, *Poopie*, *Hawkey* or *Bakey* by the locals. It's a place where sweet tea is served with every meal. The food is well seasoned and filled with love, calories, and butter. Salt and pepper are never needed. The shakers are just decorations. Although you have no room for it, homemade dessert will be offered. So, "why not have a piece or two," my family will insist. There are no fast-food restaurants. By my count, there's: one grocery store, one liquor store, one stoplight, one school, one gas station, and about a dozen churches. The residents clearly enjoy their lifelong covenant with The Lord. They live, and look good, well into their eighties, nineties, or better.

The last time I visited this part of South Carolina, was about fifteen years ago. None of the things listed above was a big enough incentive for me to make the at least ten-hour trek to go and do nothing.

But when I did, recently, one of my cousins, J.J., who drove from another part of South Carolina to see us, asked me, "What brought you to Whitmire?!"

Getting a little older, and death, had changed my perspective. I had to go visit the house in which I had spent so many summer days and nights. My parents would send me to stay for about a week during some summers growing up. I had to see my Aunt Dot. I needed to see her face, get a hug, and taste her cooking! She spent all day sipping her diet Pepsi, making salmon croquettes, grits, chicken—baked, not fried—rice, noodles, broccoli, cabbage, a coconut pie, and an almond pound cake just for us. Because she doesn't eat like that!

I had invited myself. My parents were going for a surprise ninetieth birthday party. When I found out, I casually added myself to their trip. I've been their plus-one since day one. All these years, I've thought nothing of it. When my little sister heard about the trip, she added herself, too. With my youngest son, who brought the count to five, we opted to rent something a little larger and more comfortable than our sedan for the trip. My dad had to be convinced that a minivan was the best option for our group. Since I was little, I noticed he wanted his return to his hometown to look good. His car was always showroom clean before we left. He was worried about the impression a minivan would make on his reputation.

"What are they going to think when they see me in the minivan?" he asked everyone, instead of directing the question to someone in particular. So, no one particularly answered.

We stayed with Aunt Dot, this was less than four months after she had lost her daughter, Debbie, to cancer. I wrote about it in *Week 5—The Funeral Tapestry*. When I was a teen, she lost her mother to cancer as well. I enjoyed just sitting and listening to her talk about everything that had happened with everybody since my dad's last visit. She put a Blues record on her record player. Then, she spoke about it. She recounted her daughter's last days and weaved in how they paralleled with her mom's. I just quietly sat on the couch, listening as she retold the details about how her daughter had made peace with everyone and everything before meeting her Maker. My aunt shared it all without a tear or crack in her voice. She's a warrior; a soldier. I'm not sure they make any like her anymore!

On Sunday, we visited my Aunt and Uncle's Southern Baptist church. Apparently, my dad grew up in the same church—before he left town around sixty years prior to join the Air Force. Besides my cousin's funeral in May, this group of my family had never been to church together. We sat on the same pew. We enjoyed some old-time gospel hymns and enjoyed just being together.

I felt a peace that I hadn't felt in a very long time. It doesn't seem to be available where I live near the Nation's Capital, but I'm sure it could be found if we took a few minutes to look for it. The trip was like a pause button for my life. I enjoyed the time in my family's house and in the minivan. We rode, talked, sang, laughed, and ate together. By the end of the long weekend, my heart and belly were overly full. I had to adjust my belt twice in just four days. I'm glad I took the long trek to peace. It was well worth it.

Now, after one of her visits, I see why my mom always says, "I could stay a whole week in Whitmire."

Next time, I'd like to experience a week filled with family, solace, peace, and good eating. And maybe I'll add a few visits to the gym when I get back.

Verses:

John 16:33

Ephesians 6:23

Romans 5:1

James 3:18

Psalm 119:165

Isaiah 26:3

Mark 4:39

Challenge:

Go Exploring. Find a hidden local gem to enjoy the peace and solitude. Thank God that He has allowed a place for you to find peace.

Prayer:

*Thank You, God, for being my peace. Help me to keep
my mind stayed on You, so I can enjoy an abiding peace
in Your presence, regardless of where I am located or
what is going on. Amen!*

My Notes

WEEK 7

God's Glory Is All Around

Sometimes I have to be out of my normal environment to really be able to be amazed by God. Sometimes we are too close to the action to be able to appreciate the wonders and things that awe others in our own lives.

I felt like I was completely immersed under the sea in the Georgia Aquarium. I spent hours with my mouth hanging open, gasping, and saying, "Oh My God." These humongous, majestic creatures had my full attention. It was so amazing at times that I just stopped, stared, and could not walk. They were prepared for people like me. They have a mobile walkway in that area. This was not my first time in an aquarium, but National Aquarium – Baltimore, although amazing in its own right, had become ordinary to me. The same is true with my life—if I am honest. God has given me much to enjoy. Even people, who don't claim to believe, can see it and they call me, blessed. But I struggle to see it. I wake up and say, "Thank You." But in the back of my mind, I am still taking inventory of the little, or large in my eyes, things that could be a little better to make me just a little happier. I am not able to marvel at the wonders God is doing in my own life. I don't see growth and progress unless someone else points it out.

God speaks to me, and I hear and understand His voice. He allows me the ability to obey when I take the opportunity to listen. I am so grateful that He uses such imperfect people as myself. The creatures in the sea also show forth His Glory and Majesty for people who don't know Him yet. Maybe these creatures are what make the sea salty. None of them quoted a scripture or invited anyone to attend local church. These creatures showed the mighty hand, peace and perfect mind of God by just being who/what they were created to be. They just were. They did not put on an act or perform. What about you, are you making the world around you flavored with the right amount of salt?

The Performance

We went to the dolphin show; it was unlike anything I had seen before. The trainers were very focused on explaining to the audience the process of training. They talked about why they chose certain behaviors to teach the dolphins; things the dolphins enjoy doing but have to be shown and positively reinforced to help them to progress. They received food, special treats, and other rewards when they exhibited the right behavior. Their trainers made it fun for the dolphins, and said they understood the dolphins were volunteers.

This speaks to me as we start to become teachers for the Kingdom. We have to get to know those who we are sent to disciple. We have to listen to God—our Father—and find ways to engage and meet people where they are. Make it fun. My God is fun! Show people that you care. Our job is to follow the pattern and to love. We don't have to judge, and we cannot save. Only Jesus can do that. Find ways to love someone, today. Challenge yourself by doing something nice for a complete stranger. If that is not challenging enough, treat someone you love like you really love them. Give them something, share time with them, cook something, draw, send them a message—you know what to do. If not, ask God to show you how to be salt and light for someone.

"For God so loved the world that He gave His one and only Son, that everyone who believes in Him shall not perish but have eternal life." (John 3:16, Berean Study Bible)

Do people know that you have the Light of the Truth living inside you at all? The world should see light shining through us as we live as children of the Most High God. It should be obvious that God is Our Father by something they can observe. But this is not a show; we don't have to act sanctimonious or any of the other ways that put people off, instead of leading them to Our—everyone's—Dad. When people ask how we are doing, instead of responding, "Blessed and highly favored," why not try telling them how you *really* are feeling. Some people are never going to step foot in a church, but they can experience the Church as you decide to be God's Body in action. You can show what Heaven is like, while we are still on Earth. He has given us the keys to the Kingdom; invite someone in, who is not like you. Love them as God has loved you. Show them what God has shown you. Allow someone to marvel at God's glory through you, His creation.

Verses:

John 3:16

Galatians 6:9-10

Matthew 5:13-16

Ephesians 5:8

Colossians 4:6

Luke 14:34

John 8:12

Challenge:

Write a short list of the things God has blessed you with. These are blessings that others can easily see, and have possibly even pointed out to you, but that you have had a hard time recognizing and appreciating. Decide who you are going to show love to and how. Write it down, commit to doing it, and do it!

Prayer:

Father, thank You for blessing me more than my mind is even able to comprehend. Your Love has been so awesome, but sometimes I forget to just stand in awe of You and who You are. Lord, thank You for allowing me to slow down and rest. Thank you for Therron, he was an amazing host and tour guide, and is a wonderful friend. Thank You for removing scales from my eyes to allow me to see blessings that I was not able to perceive previously. Thank You for correcting my vision with Your touch that has healed the blind; I can see clearly now. Your prescription of Love will allow someone to see You for the first time. Use me God as a corrective lens. Allow Your Holy Spirit to shine through me and correct vision as You see fit.

We love You, in Jesus' Name we pray! Amen!

My Notes

Incredible Witness —
Indelible God

One summer, I went on vacation to celebrate Joy's birthday, she's one of my best friends. We have been friends since elementary school, and we've been going on trips together since high school. This time we stayed in a beautiful beach house in an affluent area in New York. Unfortunately, I partied too hard, drank, and became belligerent. I used the mouth, that was supposed to praise God, to spew out curse words. Apparently, I was not mean to anyone, but my mouth and actions made me look like the former me. I represented generational curses instead of the generational blessings that Jesus died to ensure I inherited.

The next morning her Cousin Candyce and others recounted the story of last night to me, that I had mostly forgotten. I was embarrassed and I felt so bad. I thought, what if someone who was there would want to buy this book but recognized me for my rant and decided not to. I was not a credible witness to anything good or holy. My living testimony, as portrayed that weekend, showed that I am more married to family ties and familiar spirits than to the Bride Groom. Good thing that was not the only defining moment in my life, and it is certainly not the end of my story.

Fortunately, He never leaves or forsakes me. He is faithful even when I am not faithful. My life should bear witness to the goodness of God. Empowered by the Holy Spirit, I have no excuse. I should not be acting a fool and standing around without His covering. I should be on duty standing in my full armor. I am called to be transformed into the very image of God. I was purchased with a price. As I have more opportunities, I will be careful to give all honor, glory, and praise with my words and actions to God. He is more than deserving of it all. I am His credible witness because He deems me worthy.

"It's not hard to do the right thing. It's hard trying to turn the wrong thing into the right thing." –Suzanne (I think, lol!)

Verses:

John 3:34

Isaiah 41:9

Isaiah 44:8

Isaiah 45:4-7

Isaiah 46:10

1 John 1:9-10

Psalm 32: 1-2 (Read the whole chapter.)

Challenge:

Read Psalm Ch 32. Think about one of the days when your thoughts, words, or actions didn't represent Our Father in Heaven well. Be bold enough to write down the account. Take away the power of the accuser by admitting your guilty status and accepting the correction that comes along with it. Allow God to show you how you are still His credible witness, even when you think you have failed Him.

Prayer:

God, thank You for loving me perfectly! Thank You for allowing me to go on vacation, although You knew my actions wouldn't represent You well. Next time when the spotlight is on me, I'm hopeful to be salt and light. Empowered by the Holy Spirit, please allow me to show You honor, glory, and dominion. Amen!

My Notes

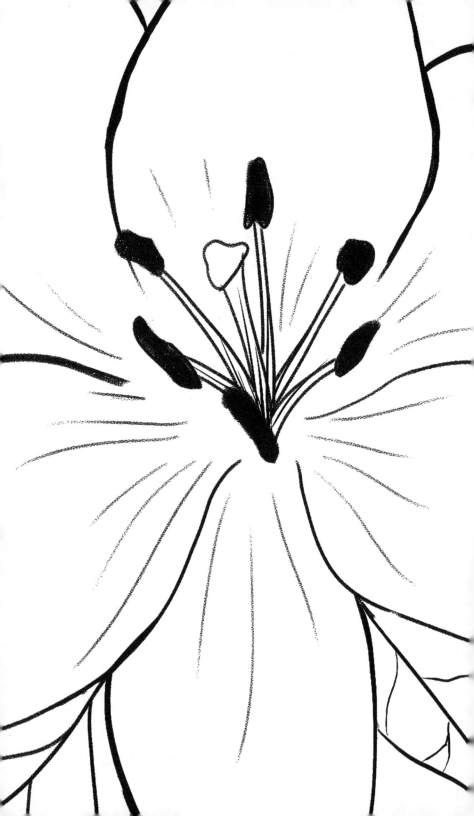

WEEK 9

Come Out Into
the Deep With Me

I was very fortunate to go to Ocean City one summer with my sons. I love being in the water. I feel like it recharges me. My younger son reminded me of myself when I was little. I remember screaming every time I was hit, or even thought I may be hit by a wave. Most trips I would even lose my voice for a while, because of all the yelling.

My youngest son tried to stay closer to the shore. He was determined not to be moved by the waves. He even mentioned digging in his heels; he wanted to fight. The waves are much more volatile at the shore. You feel the push of the new wave and a pull from an old wave going back to sea. Many times, he got knocked down and was scraped by the jagged debris that got washed up to the shore.

My solution was to have him come closer to me. "Oh no mom, do you see how tall the water is? The waves are higher! No, I can't do that!" he protested.

I tried to show him how to navigate the waves. I told him to jump or swim a little when they come. Of course, the wave may sweep you off your feet, but you can just ride the wave! He still wasn't convinced and spent only a little time enjoying the water. I wanted him to enjoy the water as much as I did. But he continued to be tossed and knocked to his knees.

What about you? Is there an area that God wants you to dive all the way into, but you just want to stay safe at the shore? Do you feel like you are having a hard-enough time just trying to stand your ground, while feeling the pull of the world against the push of God? Is there something He has asked you to do, but you have carefully calculated the very least that you can do to be *obedient*? Are you really being obedient? Or are complying only in a tight-fisted way?

He wants to change our heart to be more like His. That conversation He is leading you to, may cause some internal waves. Forgiveness may seem too deep. The money may seem short as bills are piling high. But these situations can reveal your idol to you. The sea belongs to God. If He calls you to go deep, please go. Not tip toe, knee, or waist deep; go all the way with Him! Some waves seem much bigger than they are. Some are big and suck you in but provide a nice ride. I can't say I didn't feel the burn of water up my nose a few times while I was out there. But I was never knocked to the ground and I truly enjoyed my experience.

Verses:

Matthew 14:27-31

Psalm 94:18-19

Luke 1:50

Jeremiah 17:7-8

Isaiah 43:2

Ezekiel 47:3-6

Job 10:17

Challenge:

Ask God to reveal the area(s) in which you need to let Him be Lord. Also ask Him to help you see the areas that best illustrate your full commitment to Him.

Prayer:

Lord, please help me to see me from Your perspective. You know my thoughts and motives even better than I do myself. Thank You for allowing me to be devoted in some areas of my life and encouraging me in the other areas where I still need to let go of false security. Help me to trust You fully as I go all the way into the deep with You.
Amen!

My Notes

WEEK 10

D'evil, devil, Satan and Santa

According to a "Did you know" facts on *Webster.com*, adversary is from the Latin adjective adversaries—turned toward.

The enemy, your opponent, may deserve a further look if only for today. In many sects of the Jewish faith there is no devil, but Satan. Satan is an angel that works for God. He provides adverse situations for our growth and development. This is supported in the Bible, the devil, Satan, has to speak to God before acting (See Job 1:6-12). This is part of how God works things together for the good of them that love Him and are called to His purpose. Since I read this earlier this year, I find Satan to be less menacing and mystical, but still very real.

This new view has really allowed me to check what is in my heart. In adverse situations, is God just handing me over to d'evil— the evil— that lives in me? Are my lusts and desires causing these undesired consequences in my life? When I take a close look at my opponent, does she look more like me than any horned, spiked-tailed fairy, or beast? What if the devil only attempts to show us what our flesh truly desires?

I believe that God works to make us like Him. It seems to be a whatever-it-takes process to get us to what He designed and predestined us to be—His Body.

Another question is, "Do we want The Creator or only His creations, like He is Santa?" You know the big, bearded guy, upstairs, up north, the North Pole? He supposed to give you your whole wish list because you've been good, right?! Take a close look in the mirror, take a magnifying glass, ask God to use His microscope and really search your heart. Give Him permission to remove anything that is not like Him and fill you with more of the Holy Spirit.

Jesus was tempted but didn't fail the test— it was truly in His heart to do the Will of the Father. He worshipped in Spirit and in Truth. What does your spirit speak in adverse times? Do those times turn you toward God? Do they drive you into a deeper relationship or farther away from your only Help?

Verses:

Genesis 50:20

Job 1:6-12

Romans 1:18-32

1 Peter 5:8-11

Psalm 97:10

1 Corinthians 5:5

1 Timothy 1:20

Challenge:

This week really try to identify your adversary and see him or her in a different light. Allow difficult and adverse times to turn you toward God, Our Father. Let Him talk to you about your purpose and the training that the adversary is providing for you in this season.

Prayer:

Dear God, please reveal me to me. Please allow me to see what is in my heart as You see it. Please cleanse me from thoughts or anything else that does not align with You. I am willing to go through whatever it takes to be Your Body, Your Church, and Your Bride. Amen!

My Notes

WEEK 11

Somebody Prayed for Me –
A Prayer Request Dream

I had a dream I was in a church conference of some sort at an unfamiliar church. At the end of service, there was a box filled with anonymous prayer requests. I picked one up and immediately, I recognized my little sister's handwriting. She also put her name, Jasmine, on the paper, in case there was any doubt in my mind. I read the issue that she said she needed prayer for and that is how the dream ended.

I woke and said a prayer for her regarding that specific issue. I also added a general prayer. Later, I texted her and told her some details of my dream. To my surprise, she said the issue was true. We spoke and I hope I instilled the words of wisdom needed for her to overcome the situation. I also let her know that I was praying for her.

God knows us very well! He also knows and sees our situations before we can even perceive them. I believe God allowed me and her to experience this situation to assure us that He is always mindful of us. We have to understand that God is never shocked or surprised by what He has allowed us to go through. In fact, He makes perfect preparations to ensure we can overcome any adversity. He intercedes on our behalf and will send one of His prayer warriors in as needed. Many times, He has dropped people into my spirit to pray for without knowing the details of their situation. He has also sent people to pray on my behalf.

"When the last days come, I will give my Spirit to everyone. Your sons and daughters will prophesy. Your young men will see visions, and your old men will have dreams." (Acts 2:17, CEV)

I sense these are last days' times, but does this passage also mean I'm an old man?

Verses:

Acts 2:17

Joel 2:28-29

Matthew 6:9-13

Romans 8:26-27

Ephesians 6:18

Matthew 26:41

Psalm 141:2

Challenge:

Pray and watch! Be aware and mindful of those around us who need our prayers. Don't wait for someone to come to you and ask. If you see the need, pray. Pray that their ears are opened to hear from God about their protection, wisdom, health, and whatever else God places in your heart at the time. Then see if He wants you to offer to pray with him or her, directly.

Prayer:

What A Mighty God! Please keep talking to me in my sleep, Father. At least I know I won't try to out talk You while I am sleeping. Thank You for anointing and equipping me for what You brought me here to do. Thank You for causing others to be moved to pray for me. The prayers of the righteous have availed much and helped me to find my way. There were times when I was so lost that I didn't even realize I was lost. Lord, please place the names of those who need prayer in my spirit. Thank You, Jesus, for interceding for me, Yourself, as the Most High Priest! Amen!

My Notes

Caged or Free

I asked God to talk to me during a recent walk in Watkins Regional Park located in Upper Marlboro, MD. He brought the animals to my attention. As I turned a corner, I saw a few enormous cows just a few feet away from me. There was only a short wooden fence, the kind that is about three feet high and only has two horizontal slats between the end posts of each section as a barrier. It struck a little fear in my heart to see an animal, almost as tall as me while on all fours, so close with no real protection between me and it. *Okay, when was the last time I've heard of a cow attacking and killing someone?* was the thought that put my mind back at ease. One cow seemed a little alarmed by my presence, too, but then it just continued to eat like the rest of the cows.

Then I heard some squirrels in the park. They sometimes unnerve me too because I think they are deer. But squirrels are much quicker and louder than deer. Deer scare the heck out of me. There are plenty in my neighborhood, but something in their stature and strength just frightens me. Do I think they are malicious and are going to attack? Not really, but I've seen the damage they can do to a car and sometimes they just get back up and keep going. That is powerful. As Christians, we should be powerful. We should face a situation that could kill us and get up and keep moving. They also know no boundaries. During a previous walk, my friend witnessed a deer jump over a six-foot gate without even a running start. They are not confined by the man-made boundaries in the park. They see them, overcome them, and keep moving.

Are we feeling secure in chains and afraid of freedom? What about you, my dear? Are you letting man-made obstacles stop your pursuit? Do you have your head down and are you just merely eating and not aware of what's going on around you? Meaning, do you go to church, read the Word, and pray for yourself, only? Are you aware when someone around you needs to be fed, needs an encouraging word or prayer? Are you cognizant enough to be able to go to the Father on someone else's behalf without them having to tell you their business and petition a prayer request from you? We have to be on the watch for opportunities to be a blessing to others and to love others like we have been commanded to do.

Are you truly caged or free? What are you doing with your freedom?

Verses:

John 8:31-36

Psalm 102:19-21

Galatians 5:1

Isaiah 61:1

Zechariah 3:7

Matthew 10:8

Luke 4:18

Challenge:

Share your story of freedom. Allow your testimony to be the healing balm that allows someone to see how God has worked in your life, and how He is willing and able to do the same for him or her. Help someone else fight; be a midwife for someone who feels that he or she is in a situation that seems to have no way out. Be the boost someone needs to leap over a hurdle or wall.

Prayer:

God, thank You for Your Son who came to set captives free! Please show me to whom I can tell my story, that it may help them overcome what You have helped me to overcome. Don't allow me to be ashamed of situations that show Your glory through my imperfections. Allow me to use my freedom to help free someone else. I am willing to do my part! Amen!

My Notes

WEEK 13

Unconditional Trust

To love is to be patient and kind, along with everything else written in 1 Corinthians 13. Unconditional love that stands the tests of time, is long suffering and never fails. As Christians we speak about unconditional love, but what about trust?

Do we trust God only when things make sense to us, or do we really trust that He is able to work all things together for the good of those who are called by His purpose and love Him? Do we trust that God has been God for a very long time and is excellent in all He does? Do we trust that He has placed the right people in the right places and will always supply all our needs?

Or do we only trust ourselves? The one who has led you astray, knocked you down, lied to you, misconceived the truth, and broken your heart. Do we only trust what we can experience with our own senses and validate with our knowledge and wisdom? Do we trust our eyesight that may be off, and our vantage point which may be skewed?

Even in disappointing situations, My Father has ensured that all my needs, and honestly, most desires are provided. The packaging or timing may not be how I expected, but I am amazed at how well He is always able to pull things together. He sees all. And knows all. And He sees me and knows me. I believe unconditional trust may be God's love language. I am learning to trust, unconditionally. I am taking the stance, wherever He goes I will follow! He is with me through it all and He is more than able to sustain me—really with an abundance!

Trust this, God has placed many treasures in you, and they will probably be enough for you to live a good life. However, don't miss out on the relationship with others. He has given them gifts to complement your gifts, and this can cause multiplication instead of simple addition. Trust God to point out the coworkers in the Kingdom who will help you to complete your assignment, then trust them with your gifts.

Verses:

Deuteronomy 1:32

Proverbs 3:5-6

Psalm 119:41-42

2 Kings 18:5

2 Chronicles 20:20

1 Corinthians 7:7

Philippians 4:1-3

Challenge:

Find and write your favorite scripture on trusting God. Note a current situation where He is allowing you to trust Him, totally. As an extra bonus, read 1 Corinthians 13.

Prayer:

Lord, please help me through the Holy Spirit to trust You completely. Please teach me how not to lean on my own understanding, according to Proverbs 3:5. Amen!

My Notes

WEEK 14

If I Take My Job As the Garden of Eden

I don't have to eat from the tree of the knowledge of good and evil.

I don't have to know what's going on behind the scenes.

I just need to enjoy the scenery that I've been given.

For a while, I began to second guess a wonderful blessing God had given me. Of course, any job has some people or situations that we may not feel are favorable, but it really seemed like I had begun to search out these things. I was taught by experience and others to be constantly on watch and expect something negative. "It's always something." Right?! The hours, flexibility, manager, and workload were all better than I could even imagine or ask for, but somehow, I started to fixate on what was wrong.

Man, my coworker can be annoying. I wonder if this business or client are ethical? Why didn't I get invited to that meeting?

I am sure you can add more from some of your past or current job experiences. My mind started wandering and it made it hard for me to enjoy what was given.

I had to be taught how to enjoy my garden-situation. I had to learn to see good and not look for bad. If God really wants me to be aware of something, in particular, He will bring it to my attention. He didn't call me to be a detective, He called me to be salt and light.

Has God given you something wonderful to enjoy, but you can't help thinking about the bad instead of the good? Are you intensely trying to figure out what is going on behind the scenes? Do you completely trust that God can give you a good blessing? Is there an area of your life that He just wants you to let go, trust Him, and enjoy?

Do you need to say?

I don't have to eat from the tree of the knowledge of good and evil.

I don't have to know what's going on behind the scenes.

I just need to enjoy the scenery that I've been given.

Verses:

Proverbs 3:7

Ecclesiastes 2:5

Genesis 2:15-17

Song of Solomon 8:13

Isaiah 1:29

Isaiah 51:3

Isaiah 61:11

Challenge:

Identify what the tree of knowledge of good and evil is for you (i.e., what is taking up your mental space). Next, identify five good aspects that surround the situation or person to fix your mind on, whenever it wants to wander into what else is going on behind the closed scenes. Tend to your garden!

Prayer:

Lord, please help me to be content. Help me to lean more into You and to stay in my lane. I don't have to know everything; I just have to know Who You are and follow what You have directed me to do. I thank You for all You give to me. I am undeserving, but so glad that You chose to show Your love to me in this manner. I love You! Amen!

My Notes

WEEK 15

To Senegal With Love

Several years ago, I was cleaning, and I sat out several large bags of trash on the curb. A little while later, I opened my front door and saw a lady from another country going through my trash. I was shocked, confused, concerned, and then I got a little angry! *How dare someone go through my trash!* I thought. I watched for a few minutes noticing how she was carefully placing half-broken toys to one side and a pile of clothes to the other. I had thrown away some things that were very damaged or ruined in my eyes for whatever reason. She seemed very excited to find clothes in the bag. I went out and gave her a trash bag. She said in limited English that she was going to put everything back, but also mentioned the clothes in the bag. I told her that I had bagged some clothes to give away and I went in the house to get those for her. She was very grateful and gladly took those along with the discarded clothes as well.

For several years, until she moved, I dropped off more bags of clothes to her. Her English became much more fluent. Over the time she told me about her village, her daughter who was there, how poor everyone was, and how grateful they all were. She also shared that many have cried with appreciation of things I have discarded. How dare I be indignant about my trash—others have viewed it as treasure?! It took this situation to change my view and to encourage me to continue to do my small part to help. I said a small prayer over the clothes that I sent.

Please keep the villages in Senegal, and the people all over the world who are less fortunate than we are, in prayer. Try to remember that your trash and the things we all find to complain about can literally be someone else's treasure. Also, keep in mind that the Father loves all of us, even those we may consider untouchable or undesirable.

I was listening to a message recently, where the preacher mentioned that she was being hosted in a foreign country. The residents of this house where she felt the Holy Spirit tangibly, mentioned how much they pray for us in America. She was told that because we have the material resources that they lack, they are praying that we are still able to know God in a similar manner as they do. They have a different understanding of what it means to know that He provides every need. They know Him, intimately, as Provider and so much more.

Verses:

2 Corinthians 4:7-12

Ephesians 2:10

Matthew 6:2-4 & 19-21

Proverbs 31:20

Galatians 2:10

Matthew 19:21

1 Corinthians 4:12-13

Challenge:

Ask God to open your eyes to see the treasure, He has placed in someone, in whom you struggle to see value. After you've done that, ask God to show you an aspect of yourself that you've tried to sweep under the rug as invaluable or unworthy.

Prayer:

Father, please help to change my view to Yours. I desire to see the treasure You have put into others. Forgive me for those times when I have looked down on others based on their current situations or past. Please help me to value the whole Body, just as You do. Thank You for pouring treasure into this earthen vessel! Allow my life to be a potent testimony for someone else. Show Your glory through my cracks, deficiencies, and issues. Amen!

My Notes

WEEK 16

New Hire—No Training

There has been a constant pattern in my life. I start jobs or have a new experience and receive little-to-no training. As I stand, blank-faced, I've been told:

"Everyone gets a week-long orientation here."

Or, "I didn't see you at the mandatory new hire training."

Or, "Just ask your new hire mentor!"

I received neither the training, the orientation, nor the mentor!

After experiencing this several times, I had to have a talk with My Father about it. He basically explained to me that there are going to be things that He has designed me to do where there will be only one human example, mentor or role model for—Jesus Christ. I have the Bible to show me what it looks like to live the type of life He is expecting me to live. His expectation is based on who He is and who I am in Him. He is God and I am His daughter. I can do all things because He strengthens me, He leads me, and He guides me. I won't be able to study man to achieve my destiny, I have to study God through the gift that Jesus has given.

Recently, I've been more interested in my gifts and how God wants me to use them. In my mind, I would like to have a mentor who has done everything that I am supposed to do, who can walk me through every step. This is unrealistic and obviously not the case. He has allowed me to cross paths with people who have some knowledge and wisdom to assist me in growing in certain areas. He has also led me to books that are helpful in my training. But I have been shown how important it is to just spend time with the Father and let Him conduct the trainings as He sees fit.

While watching a movie this line was highlighted to me, "We train you like we do to teach you to never give up." - From the movie *Divergent*

Verses:

John 13:15

2 Timothy 3:16-17

Romans 15:4

Proverbs 4:1-7

John 14:26

Revelation 1:1-3

1 John 2:27

Challenge:

Identify one or more of your gifts. Spend some time with God. Ask Him to assign a book of the Bible to help with developing your gift for His Glory. Be a willing partner in the training He gives you. In the weeks to come, use your gift for someone else's benefit.

Prayer:

God, please help me to realize that I need You to train me in the way that I should go. Allow me to use my gifts for the benefit of my neighbor and give me the opportunity to pass the love You have shown me to them as well. Let the blessings You have given me be a true blessing to someone else. Help me not to hide or be fearful of my gifts. Allow me to use them generously for Your Glory. I thank You, love You, and appreciate my gifts and talents! Amen!

My Notes

WEEK 17

The Warrior Bride

Are you a Spiritual gangster? What about when The Kingdom enemies: Python, Leviathan, and Jezebel (P. L. J.) try to run roughshod on you? Running you through your greatest failures. Reminding you of every time you've been let down. Bringing up every time you've felt lonely. Drowning you in every negative thought and emotion in your history.

"From the days of John the Baptist until now the kingdom of heaven has suffered violence, and the violent take it by force." (Matthew 11:12, ESV)

"God, please help me, God please help me!" was all I could muster between gasps for oxygen. 'P' was squeezing all the life out of me. All its eggs had hatched. 'L' had his teeth set against me. He went for the jugular with carefully delivered insults. 'J' wove a web of word curses telling me who she thought I was. Little did they know that no weapon formed against me shall prosper!

"Sister, please pray for me," and she did. Patricia's name means noble and she has fulfilled that and so many other beautiful characteristics. Although we share the same last name, we aren't blood relatives. I have tasted the fruit, tried it, and know that beyond the Washington, D.C. and P.G. exterior (P.G. is how locals refer to Prince George's County—the county in which I was also reared), she is as sweet as they come. Reminding me of the rambutan which she brought me and Helen one day. We sat and enjoyed God's splendor at a, previously unknown to me, local mini paradise fully equipped with shady trees and a lake.

Her prayer was short, piercing, and effectual. Just like the prayers of the righteous should be. She let me catch my breath and see clearly who God had already told me I was. My other sister, Jasmine, painted a picture that includes Words that I see every morning. A beautiful melanin-rich princess is adorned in a head wrap that has joy, peace, chosen, forgiven, and several other attributes that He has spoken into her earthen vessel. I agreed with those words and then remembered others that He has spoken directly to me over the years.

Wait a minute! The words of 'P' and 'L' and 'J' that kept coming for me were contrary to what God had spoken and had brought back to my remembrance. That means this was an attack of the enemy. Oh, I've got something for this. In the Name of Jesus, I came against all the attacks, schemes of the devil, and the demonic. I called out a few that I know have plagued me during my journey in general, but specifically in my quest to complete this book.

I went from thinking I can't breathe to experience life-giving breath, peace and freedom. Thank You, God! You have no worthy opponents. Only defeated foes.

I cleaned up some things to which I needed to attend, to bring decency and order to my bedroom. I praised God for all He does for me, my friends, family, loved ones, and even my enemies. They need God's love, too. It is the only way to repentance and right relationship with God.

I was then told to send a message equipping a young warrior for her day. So, I did. When I got back to a video that I was watching I was told to look at the time elapsed. I did. I looked up the number in *Strong's Concordance*. It meant risk, disregard in Greek and flame, blade in Hebrew. That sounded powerful, but then I read the verses associated with it.

It stopped in my tracks and started praising God even more, when I got to Job 41:13 and realized this is the chapter where 'L' is spoken about in detail. I don't have a lot of worldly wisdom about this high-ranking demon. But I do know he is one of the major enemies of the Kingdom that has been plaguing me since I agreed to write this book. And he's attempted to halt my opportunities to be a prophetic voice.

The enemy's schemes are no match for the Almighty God. He is My Father, My Shepherd, and My Guide. I felt so free and delivered. Renewed in Him. Powerful, blessed, blossoming, beautiful—like the warrior bride that He has told me I am.

I called my surrogate sister, Patricia, and thanked her for being a willing vessel. I messaged my other sister, "Your painting helped my mind, body, soul and spirit on today. Bless those beautiful little hands in Jesus' Name, Amen." They were used by God to set this captive free. We each have a choice to be in unison with the spirit in which we choose to operate. I choose love and life with the Holy Spirit.

Verses:

Revelation 2:18-23

2 Kings 9:22,30-37

Job 41:13

Isaiah 27:1

Psalm 74:12-13

Leviticus 20:27

Acts 16:16

Challenge:

Read more about these Kingdom Enemies on phyllisfordministries.com. These dark forces are powerful and real. But they are defeated—powerless to Our Mighty Battle-ax.

Prayer:

Catch fire and be burned in the eternal pits of Hell, 'P', 'L', 'J'. Jesus rebukes you, Satan! In Jesus' mighty Name I pray and believe! Amen!

My Notes

WEEK 18

Be Full in the Fruit of the Spirit — Multiply Spiritually

Have you ever wondered why God told us to be fruitful? Why does He show a comparison or likeness to fruit? I have been thinking about that a lot, while in my little garden. What is special about fruit? For the most part, fruit is sweet, refreshing, and has the seed. The seed gives the fruit the ability to produce more like it, when placed in the correct environment for growth. A tomato can grow from a seed and it will produce many tomatoes, each containing many seeds. Each one of those seeds has the ability to accomplish the same multiple results of the first.

With a bag of chips, I can eat them and have an empty bag at the end to throw away or recycle. We live in a society where most things are packaged; they look nice but there is nothing but death in it. It is like the whitewashed tombs we read about.

"You Pharisees and teachers are in for trouble! You're nothing but show-offs.

You're like tombs that have been whitewashed. On the outside they are beautiful, but inside they are full of bones and filth. That's what you are like. Outside you look good, but inside you are evil and only pretend to be good." (Matthew 23:27-28, CEV)

We are to be like fruit, allowing nourishment, replenishment, and multiplication. The connection to God allows us to produce much good fruit. God changes us, which changes others. People are supposed to be forever changed after receiving a seed of the Spirit that should be living inside of us. They shouldn't have to continuously come back to us as the source, but they should always know that God is the Source. As we lift God, He will draw all men to Himself with the sweetness of the fruit of the Spirit. He calls Himself *Living Water* and *Living Bread*. He calls us to be the same. He doesn't call us to be packaged, but alive, connected to the True Vine and life-giving. We have a choice: Are we going to be life giving with the fruit of The Spirit or are we going to be life taking like pre-packaged products?

Verses:

Genesis 1:22, 26-28

Genesis 9:1-7

Genesis 17:1-8 (Read the whole chapter.)

Ezekiel 47:12

Proverbs 1:30-33

John 15:1-6

Revelation 22:2

Challenge:

There are so many fruitful characteristics that Christians should share with others. Find some examples in the Bible and/or in your life experiences. Recall last week, how did you take the opportunity to be good fruit for someone else? Were you willing to give away a seed or did you just give them a taste or teaser testimony? Take the opportunity this week to be fruitful.

Prayer:

God, thank You for being the True Vine and thank You for planting a seed in me. Since You are the Gardener Who provides the increase, I know that the seed will not fail. I know that You are working to produce a healthy harvest in and through my life, that will produce good fruit with a potent seed. I want my fruit to be like Your Son's. His fruit left people forever changed and with permanent access to You. I give my life to You to do as You will. I am willing to put my flesh to death for Your Kingdom and to provide fertile ground for Your spiritual Seed. Holy Spirit, help me to live this conviction daily, in Jesus' Name! Amen.

My Notes

WEEK 19

The Flood Dream

In my dream, I left my house and had a bag of clothes to bring to another house in my neighborhood, which was known as a *family house*. I'm not sure exactly who lived in the house, but it's just a house for family members to live in as needed or wanted, and for family gatherings. I turned onto the street of the family house.

It started to rain harder and harder. I parked a few houses down the street, which was on a hill. The water was coming down so fast from the sky and pouring down the street. The street began to flood. Then there was a lot of brown water raising up and covering my car. I saw cars being washed down the street toward my car. At this point, I put on the emergency break and I was praying. I was concerned that another car may hit my car, my car may be washed away, I may drown, or some other unwanted scenario.

Then just as suddenly as the rain had started, it stopped. The water stopped flowing on the street and I decided to get my bags and walk up toward the house. I passed a few people on this cobblestone street, some I recognized and some I didn't. I noticed some cars had been moved down the street because of the flood. On the street there were just car pieces, like the leftovers of a bad accident; some cars were destroyed. But I noticed, none of the houses were damaged. I went in the house, there were a lot of family members there. I hugged everyone, including the

Clemons family (from my sons' first homeschool co-op, Children of the Sun). When I saw my mom, she was very worked up because of the flood and damage. I tried not to feel overwhelmed, I was thinking everyone was fine and only cars have been damaged. The dream ended shortly after.

During this same time, Louisiana was being ravished with floods. I shared the dream with my older sister, Shani. She said she thought those houses were built on The Rock; that was wisdom speaking. I shared the dream again at a Bible Study a couple of nights later. We read from Luke 6 in part, but I had the urge to keep reading until I reached verse 46 and continued to 49. The story of the wise and foolish builders gave me more insight into the dream. Our faith must be built on the Chief Cornerstone. All the rest is built on sinking sand. The cars seemed to represent those who are tossed to-and-fro, carried by every wind of doctrine. There are people in the Body at all different stages of maturity. At a time, such as this, not only should we be hearers of the Word, but also doers. We also need to allow the words of our testimony to aid others in overcoming hardships of their journey.

Verses:

Luke 6:46-49

Psalm 9:9

Matthew 7:24-27

Psalm 62:7-8

Psalm 32:6

Psalm 46:1

Ephesians 4:14

Challenge:

Is there an adverse area in your life that you've just become aware of or just got delivered from? Consider that God made that deficiency in your life large enough for you to realize that only He can fill it. Be willing to share your powerful overcoming testimony with others.

Prayer:

Father, please allow things that I have gathered in the name of religion to be washed away. Allow my foundation to be solid in You, the Stone the builders rejected. Thank You for allowing me to dwell in Your secret place. Please allow my testimony to be useful to The Kingdom! Amen!

My Notes

WEEK 20

There's a Monster in My Closet—The Death of Fear

One night, I watched a prophetic video encouraging believers to spend unrestricted time with God to allow Him to do whatever needs to be done in us and through us. I felt a real urge to pull out my *war room* board and pray. My son prayed first. Then as I started, there was a loud rattling noise in or near my closet for at least thirty seconds straight. I hopped up, confused, and was like, *What in the world?!* We looked around the room a little while. The only thing we saw was a small beetle on a bag in my room, which I promptly killed. I was thinking that was not the source of that large noise. But I decided to go back to praying without further investigation of the noise and its source.

The prayer was even more powerful after that. It even moved me to tears. I asked God to take doubt, fear, and unbelief from me. I asked that He would allow me to trust in the manner that is pleasing to Him. I felt like my prayer was immediately answered. I stayed in my room with no fear. My son actually stayed with me, too. We never found the source of the noise and honestly, we didn't try to look very hard. I slept, confidently, in the presence of the Almighty God!

Shortly after this night, I remember that I saw a very long snake that took up most of a street lane. Snakes used to be a very big fear of mine. I didn't feel fear when I saw it, maybe because I was in an SUV or maybe because my armor was on.

I have had to make decisions in situations with many unknowns. How do I really know if this is the best school for my child? Is this the best career path? Should I take them to the doctor now or wait a couple more days? I have had a fear of picking the wrong thing because of lack of wisdom in an area. I have made many costly mistakes that God, of course, has walked with me or carried me through. God has allowed me to make my mistakes while still being Sovereign.

Another fear that I had to deal with was spiders! For several weeks, I would see three to five spiders a day inside the house. I used to just scream and ask someone else to get it. But I killed each of these without assistance and got pretty good at getting them with the first blow. One night, I even had to kill a rather large spider with a shovel that was inside the screen door.

He is also helping me to conquer the fear of rejection. Writing these devotionals, sharing them in the Bible Study and other ministry opportunities have really helped me in this area.

I've also had a fear of death! I had been fortunate to not have death sting the family but once in a ten-year span, until recently. In 2017 that streak was broken, and I have felt the pain of losing loved ones. My cousin and faithful servant, Pastor Lumbus T. Burrell, was called home. It was hard, but not as bad as I had feared. I also was able to see something beautiful. The Body was functioning as the Bride. It was a co-laborer with God, bringing healing, comfort, and Heaven to Earth.

My fears in each situation have proven to be worse than actually experiencing what I feared would happen. Good riddance to doubt, fear, and unbelief. They can't rest in peace, nor abide, here. They must be bound up and sent back to the pits of Hell where they belong.

Verses:

Psalm 4:8

Psalm 27:1-5

Psalm 56:3-4

Psalm 91:1-2

Psalm 118:6

Isaiah 41:10

2 Timothy 1:7

Challenge:

Commit to do something that you have previously been afraid to do. You can use the following format: Today, I will_____.

Prayer:

By the power in Jesus' Name, all doubt, fear, and unbelief be gone! God, allow me to trust You, completely. With power, love, and a strong mind I will stand courageous knowing You are always with me, in Jesus' Name I pray! Amen!

My Notes

WEEK 21

Saints, Please Open Your Bible and Follow Me to Nahum

How often have you been asked to turn to Nahum? If asked, would you be able to find it in your Bible? (Online and App versions don't count.) In church, there are several books of the Bible to which we are rarely directed. What are the books of the Bible that you've never read?

My list includes the following:

Verses:

Nahum

Haggai

Songs of Solomon

Zephaniah

Jude

Titus

Philemon

Challenge:

List up to seven books of the Bible that you've never read, or aren't familiar with. See how God reveals Himself to you in those books. Take one book from your list and write a one-page summary or think of a creative way to share with others what you've learned.

Prayer:

Heavenly Father, please reveal Yourself to me with the help of the Holy Spirit through Your Word. Add more to our arsenal as we discover books of the Bible with which we're not familiar. Help us to explore the Full Gospel of Your Kingdom message that exists throughout the entire Bible, not just the popular verses. Amen!

My Notes

WEEK 22

Faith — Flying Without Mirrors

When my sons and I went out to dinner, my oldest noticed there was a corner mirror positioned for wait staff as they entered and exited the kitchen. Years ago, we went to another restaurant where the staff had to constantly call out, "corner," to alert everyone that they were coming around the corner. Due to the design of the restaurant, and the high walls of its booths, there was no way to tell if the coast was clear without the call.

On Labor Day 2016, I woke up to multiple unexpected blessings in our family and family business. We have three generations of visual artists in the family. We display art and teach art classes in our community as *The Jackson Family Art Show*. Our first-generation artist, and my uncle, C.R. Wells, was featured in the local paper, *The Washington Post*, in an article about minimum wage not being an adequate living wage. Subsequently, he received more than $10,000 in sales, gifts, and donations. The generosity changed our perception on the level of empathy in the world. It also provided resources for my uncle's needs to be met and for us to continue offering art classes, locally.

Often, God has been assuring me of the blessings He is preparing me for in my future. I can feel things coming, but I can't see or know what is next. He didn't ask me to predict what was coming; He asked me to prepare. There is no way to see what is coming around the corner, and we don't need to either.

God is equipping and preparing us better than we can imagine or pretend we have the ability to do by ourselves. All we really need to do is listen and follow instructions. Something good is coming, it's right around the corner! Trust that God can see what that is, and that He knows how to prepare us for everything else—from everlasting to everlasting.

Verses:

Galatians 2:20

Romans 1:17

Mark 10:52

2 Corinthians 5:7

Psalm 119:30

Hebrews 11:6-7, 39-40 (Read the whole chapter.)

James 2:14-26

Challenge:

Live by faith and not by sight. This week acknowledge your feelings and what you see, but act on and believe only in what God reveals to you!

Prayer:

Thank You, Father, for being the Master Planner. Thank You for ensuring I have a part in this awesome creation! Please help me to listen to You, hear clearly, and quickly obey. Please correct me if I overthink. Please help me to understand that You are always for me. Help me to be a part of Your unified Body—following the leadings of Our Head, Jesus Christ! You are amazing, I love You! Amen!

My Notes

WEEK 23

Thinning — Solitary Refinement

We have green beans as one of our crops. The beans were sowed three seeds per hole and just a few inches from the next hole. Once the sprouts reached about three inches, we were to thin the sprouts. I had never heard of this before, so I had to look it up.

According to *Interested in Growing Green Beans? On the Backyard Vegetable Gardening* website, thinning plants means, "selectively removing seedlings. If the plants are growing too close together, problems may arise. The root systems will end up growing into each other. When plants have to battle each other for water and nutrients, they end up becoming stressed and rarely grow to full size or produce green beans. To solve this problem, seedlings are thinned to create adequate space between the plants." I read something else that stated that, "thinning is necessary, so the sprouts are not fighting for sun, nutrients and other things required for the plant to bear fruit." This spoke to me on a spiritual level.

Sometimes God has called me to be alone with Him, to a place where no one can quite understand what He is doing. No one can validate what I have heard from Him, but Him. This place can feel lonely, but God is always there. I could not understand why we should plant three seeds in the same hole if we just have to dig them up and thin them later. Why not just plant them separately in the beginning? I didn't look that up, but you can if you feel led.

In *Week 3—God Still Speaks—On Trial,* I shared how I have attended a few churches in my life and now I am being homeschooled. Maybe it didn't cause you to ask questions, but I did ask and have received some answers. Why did I have to leave my first church; I thought it was perfect! I was shown love there, I got baptized there, and I was being taught the Word of God. Why was I directed to leave my family's church, when others were planted there for the rest of their lives? Why am I homeschooled now? I do take part in fellowships and community services, but on a less-frequent basis. And it has caused me to feel as though I am in solitary confinement sometimes, without a weekly fellowship on my calendar. However, God wanting private time shouldn't be viewed as punishment, but a privilege.

In 2020, almost the whole world has been under stay-at-home orders due to the COVID-19 Global Pandemic. Did you use that time to binge shows and movies on Netflix, Amazon or on your favorite cable channel? Did you stay up on Instagram, Twitter, another social media platform, or obsessing over the local news? Or did you use it as face time with the Father? I will not lie, I did both. But I definitely used part of the time to make some more progress on this book and to get in quality time with God.

Sometimes God has us to follow His directions without knowing why, just being certain that He is all knowing and loves us. The thinning process is for our growth, so we can bear fruit and be a blessing; not just to those in our immediate circle, but to a much larger segment of society. Are you willing to go into the secret place of the Most High to allow Him to transform you into His perfect likeness? While we are there, He will provide all that is needed!

Verses:

Psalm 27:4

Psalm 31:20

Psalm 32:7

Psalm 61:7-8

Hebrews 11:8

Mark 1:35

Matthew 6:6-8

Challenge:

Set a time and date to spend at least one hour, alone, with God. Plan to play gospel/worship songs, read, pray, be quiet, and listen (in no particular order). Bring a pen and paper to write down whatever He speaks to you or whatever is highlighted to you during this time.

Prayer:

Dear God, I thank You for the secret place. I thank You for wanting to spend time with me and refining me specifically for what You have created me for. I am grateful to know I am alive with purpose and don't have to take a one-size-fits-all approach to religion. God, You are all I need. Thank You for having a genuine relationship with me that makes me feel special and loved. And I love You, too! Amen!

My Notes

Crossing Jordan

I was inspired by a message where the preacher said he frequently gave large tips to his waiters and waitresses. Apparently, we don't do the best job as the Body to show appreciation to those who make their living servicing us. This sentiment is particularly felt on Sundays as we interact with the world after our worship services. I thought it was so neat to be able to completely change someone's outlook by simply giving a nice tip and expressing gratitude. God allowed me several of these opportunities to give. He placed a certain amount in my heart to give. Sometimes I added a small note to the effect of, "Jesus is real, and He loves you very much!"

I had two experiences with servers, named Jordan. The first was when I met for dinner, Dafnette Jones, a childhood friend and the author of an amazing book, *The Waiting Room*. The lady, who took our orders, was named Jordan. We ate at a sit down or carry-out style restaurant, so there was really no good or bad service provided. When we were ready to go, I gave her the note and money and left. A few weeks later, I was out to lunch with another friend—yes, I like food and friends. As we paid the bill, I read her name tag— Jordan.

Now, God had my attention and I had to do a little digging in the Old Testament (See Joshua 1:10-18). The Israelites had to cross the Jordan River to go into the Promised Land. Some of the land promised to certain tribes was on the east and the rest was west of the river. The stronger warriors crossed the river to help the other tribes fight the giants inhabiting the land they were promised. Once they were victorious, the tribes all went to their appointed land.

The Jordan River signifies death and resurrection. Here we can bury self-centeredness and make the decision to live life as God directs us. Living as a sacrifice, willing to tell God, "Not my will, but Your Will be done." I don't have to have things my way, I will say "yes" to Your way. "I'll go where You want me to go, I'll do what You want me to do! Yes Lord!" I know I can't be the only one who has agreed and sang these words.

God has reminded me of the whole deliverance (Exodus) story of the Israelites as He is preparing me for marriage, and other journeys. During parts of this journey, I have been led to help others in their journey. I have fasted, prayed, and encouraged other women who are also preparing for marriage, while I am in the same season. During other seasons, I've needed people who have at least made it down the aisle to encourage, speak truth to me, and help me along the way.

While you are going through your own challenging or growing seasons, what do you do? Are you willing to bring someone along and help him or her progress in their journey while you are still on your way to perfection? Or are you going to miss the opportunity to lend a hand because you don't feel like you have yet mastered this area yourself? Don't wait until you are so far removed, saved, or healed from a situation that you have lost empathy for those going through the challenge.

Be willing to speak up about what you are going through as you are still learning from it. People can be taught well from real people who are willing to share their testimony. You will probably be surprised when that person is able to add insight to your journey as well. God allows us to gain a better view when we share with others. Being myopic, and only using our singular perspective leads to a lack of depth perception. Don't miss out on this wonderful opportunity to share!

Verses:

Deuteronomy 9:1-3

Joshua 1:10-18

Joshua 3:11-17

Malachi 3:16-18

Romans 1:11-12

Romans 14:19

Revelation 12:11

Challenge:

Be a midwife, help deliver someone from what you're coming out of. Be transparent and humble enough to seek help from a mentor who has successfully made it through what you are going through. Find someone from whom you can seek help during your fight. Or give help to someone, you know is struggling during his or her fight. Your offer may be turned down, but you can only do your part. Allow God to do the rest!

Prayer:

Thank You, God, for strong warriors when I am weak as well as providing Your strength to allow me to be strong for someone else. Thank You for orchestrating opportunities for the Body to be more vulnerable and cohesive. Allow us to discern the timing of crossing into new territories and align us with the help we need. Humble us until we look just like You, Jesus! Amen!

My Notes

Genesis to Revelation

My grandmother's funeral was eye-opening for me. It was when I first recognized that she was much more than my mom's mom and my grandmother. I heard so many stories from her life before I knew her. My sisters and cousins were the only people in the gathering who even knew her as *grandma*. She made me feel so loved, I forgot that she had a life and other relationships outside of the wonderful one that we shared.

Would it be okay for someone who only knows you from church to assume they know all of you? Would they be surprised about some of the things you have enjoyed or participated in or perhaps your current guilty pleasures? Do they know every good and righteous deed you've done and every thought you've had? It's doubtful that someone can have a very limited and canned interaction and yet have a complete view of you. Their perspective is skewed.

What about God? Do you think you know all of Him by simply reading a few passages about Jesus as directed by your pastor? Do you think there may be other facets of God you need to explore on your own time? God knows everything about us and still loves us. Can we say the same? Can we know God and know that He is God over everything? He works in good and so-called bad times out of His love. As He reveals and removes scales from our eyes, as we see Him and His definition of perfect, will we still love Him, or will we be jaded?

In other words, if He stops attempting to complete your make-me-happy-today list, will you still love Him? If you feel He has taken something that you thought was yours, will you love? If He says no, will you love? They should know we are Christians by our love.

According to *Webster's Dictionary*, Genesis means origin. One of its synonyms is beginning—makes sense to me. Revelation doesn't mean end or completion, but I think I understand why the last book is named, Revelation. If we take the time to read the Bible with the Holy Spirit as our guide, it gives us the opportunity to know and experience multiple facets of God. We can decide, after all of that, if we still love and want to be with Him forever, or if we are the child who just wants the name, inheritance, promises, and blessings.

I was also thinking of the verse where God said, in part, "Depart from Me, I never knew you." He didn't say you didn't know about Me or you never knew Me. Although He knows and sees all, do you only present Him a *Sunday's Best*, limited and sanitized view of yourself? Are we willing to truly know and be known by God?

Verses:

Genesis 1:1

John 17:3

Philippians 3:7-11

1 John 5:20

John 10:14

Isaiah 54:5

Revelation 22:21

Challenge:

Spend at least an hour this week reading God's Word. Pray for the Holy Spirit to interpret for you as you read the entire chapter in which these verses are found. Note if the verses speak to you differently with more context. Write down a few revelations about God or His character that may challenge what you learned in church, picked up along the way, or limited due to prior letdowns. Share those revelations with Him. Allow Him to reveal more to you as He goes over the pages of your story with you.

Prayer:

Please forgive me for limiting my perception of You. God, we want to know all of You as You know all of us. We don't want to just have mythical fables about You, we want You! Reveal Yourself to us. Thank You for the Words that embody Your Spirit and reveal Your heart and mind. Help us to reveal our true self to You. You already know all about us. So, please help us to be open, honest, and transparent with You. Please allow the grace of the Lord Jesus to be with us all. Amen!

My Notes

WEEK 26

Three Ways to Die

The Ocean City boardwalk had some beautiful sand sculptures that blew my mind. One stood out to me in particular. It was the scene of Jesus hanging on the cross with the two criminals. LOVE was spelled out in between the crosses.

The next night we walked the beach, a couple was fishing using three poles buried in the sand. This reminded me of the sand sculpture. The gentlemen got a catch, but as he was reeling in what appeared to be feisty game, whatever was on the other end broke free. He went back near the water to cast the line again and ended up getting very wet with the next big wave.

Jesus went into many messy situations to complete His tasks. He was willing to get wet and uncomfortable for ministry. He knew the Father intimately and was willing to go the full distance to be the Fisher of Men. When He died, He granted access to Heaven for all of us through His sacrifice on the cross.

Next to Him, a convicted criminal asked Jesus to remember him. Jesus let the criminal know he would be in Paradise with Him that very day. He lived the life of a criminal but did a last-minute conversion and gained access to Heaven. But he had no ministry or testimony while he was living. The other criminal questioned who Jesus was, and died. He may have gone to Hell that night, but King Jesus went and conquered death, Hell, and the grave. I wouldn't be surprised if he is in Heaven now.

Why? Because Jesus died to grant us all the ability to access Heaven. As Christians we have a responsibility, while we are living, to show other people how to get there and to bring Heaven to Earth.

Which way will you choose to die? Will you spend your time here, serving others in ministry or serving yourself? Will you realize who God is and what Jesus has given you while you are living, on your deathbed, or afterward—when all is revealed? The choice is yours.

Verses:

Matthew 27:50-53

Luke 23:39-43

Mark 1:15-17

Matthew 4:17

Philippians 1:27-30

1 Thessalonians 2:11-13

Colossians 1:9-12

Challenge:

Decide how you are going to show someone Christ, in the same way He has revealed Himself to you. Who are you willing to forgive—knowing you are forgiven? Who will you heal—knowing you have been healed? Who will you love with a selfless and sacrificial love—just as you have been loved?

Prayer:

God, please help us to use our gifts and talents to give You glory while we still have time. Let us live in a way that show others Who You are and Who You have been to us. Please help us to walk worthy of You. Amen!

My Notes

My Purpose – A Different Type of Healing

One Sunday, I left out for church later than usual and I only brought my oldest son with me. My tank was empty, and the warning light was on. I've never figured out exactly what the flashing dashes on my screen meant, but when I see the flickering, I make sure I go to the gas station to refill. By the time my tank was filled, it was thirty minutes after my church had started and I still had a fifteen or twenty-minute ride. A small voice told me to visit another local church, so I did. The message was about Jonah and how he was attempting to run from an assignment God had given him. I kept nudging my son during the message to try to get him to focus on how this message must have pertained to him. Why else would we be there?

Later, I asked God if there was anything from which I was running. It was revealed to me that my purpose was to be a healer. I was very surprised when I heard this, but neither of my sons were. They mentioned my stockpile of supplements, herbs, oils, and ointments. Then they talked about how I never want to take them to the doctor, or go myself, if I can avoid it. If I find out anyone has an ailment, I'm researching the home remedy, and I likely have most of the ingredients already in my cabinet. During the COVID-19 Global Pandemic, I have recommended and supplied the following supplement regimen to assist the body in healing from the virus: oil of oregano, zinc, echinacea goldenseal, probiotics, air power, quercetin bromelain, and neem oil or tablets.

Okay, that made sense, now what? I learned about some different forms of healing, some interested me, but some seemed outside of my calling and the Will of God. I had a narrow view until a close friend, Lynn, told me she got a message for me to think about who or what I am to heal. I was called not only to heal the physical, but also the mind and spirit.

God also reminded me that I'm a warrior. I understood that to mean that my assignment will vary based on where He is sending me. Jesus was an awesome Healer—He touched whatever part needed healing. He also showed us how to get home, and ultimately be with God. I'm glad He widened my view.

A year or so later, I was watching a series about Jonah. I was, again, in a situation I was trying to run from. I no longer wanted to complete a task like I had promised, things had gotten complicated and messy. I was reminded not to be Jonah—not to go left when I know God is asking me to do something right.

I woke up one morning to the small voice speaking, repeating again and again about my purpose: *a healing for a people and a land*. Yes God, I'm listening, willing, and able to be obedient!

Verses:

Acts 26:16-18

Ephesians 2:10

Jonah 1:1-4 & 17

Jonah 2:7-10

Jonah 4:1-4 (You may want to read the entire book of Jonah.)

Ezekiel 33:6

Jeremiah 23:19-22 (Read the whole chapter.)

Challenge:

Ask God to show you areas in your life where you may be living like Jonah. Have you run away from a specific assignment? Have you completed an assignment without giving it your best effort? Or after all was said-and-done, did you argue with God about how whomever you helped didn't deserve His grace and mercy?

Prayer:

Please forgive me for not wanting to do Your Will—Your Way. I am sorry that I have agreed to things when they looked good, only to want to return-to-sender after things failed to fulfill my fantasy. Lord, I submit my will to You. Please exchange my will for Yours. Amen!

My Notes

WEEK 28

Wine on the Vine

I had a dream where an unfamiliar pastor, his wife, and a child were in a bed. He was helping me to make a bed for myself and my sons right beside theirs. The bed didn't look appealing. The pillows and cases were old, worn, and flat. He started to tell me what *god* told him to tell me. The pastor's voice sounded similar to one of my old pastors, but I still steadily rejected the untrue word he was speaking over me. I never ended up lying down or putting my kids to rest in the bed I had started to prepare with him.

At that time, I was thinking this dream was about an unholy trinity. I read about the number assigned to unholy trinity, as I understand, it represents the best system of governance that mankind can produce without God and under the constant influence of the chief adversary. Man's system on Earth is made up of three major parts: economic, religious, and governmental.

Now, I am considering that the dream may be about religion and religious traditions. Instead of faith, hope, and love, we are still plagued with doubt, fear, and unbelief. These aren't fruits of the Spirit, but seem to represent the dragon, the beast, and the false prophet.

When I woke up, I read the verse of the day on *Biblegateway. com.* It was:

"But seek first The Kingdom of God and His righteousness, and all these things will be added unto you." (Mathew 6:33, Berean Study Bible)

I kept reading and listening to the audio Bible. When I got to Chapter Nine, God whispered 17.

"Neither do men pour new wine into old wineskins. If they do, the skins will burst, the wine will spill, and the wineskins will be ruined. Instead, they pour new wine into new wineskins, and both are preserved." (Matthew 9:17, Berean Study Bible)

I was wondering what it meant, and then also why there is so much talk about wine in the Bible. It led me to study. I knew there is a passage about not only drinking water, but also wine for the sake of the stomach. On occasion in the past, I've quoted it to wrongly justify an overindulgence of wine. I knew water represents the Word, but what about wine? As I studied, I also kept wondering about the new wine in old wineskin verses. I had seen them plenty of times before but had no understanding of what it all meant.

I recently had grapes that sat too long before being eaten. They were well past their good and ripe state; I commented that they tasted like wine on the vine. One article I read mentioned new wine as being the ripe grape, old wine being fermented and having the ability to make us drunk. The new wine was likened to us. We are supposed to be connected to the vine, fresh, appealing and, most of all, fruit with the powerful seed of life in it. That pure and powerful seed cannot be housed in our old leathery flesh. We must die to ourselves to house that seed.

We shouldn't get drunk off of a man's word that is a dash of truth, watered down, then mixed up with a spoonful of sugar to make the medicine go down. That produces yeast. We must crave what is pure and from Our Father, only. You can't put new ideas into old mindsets. You can't get new results by instituting old behaviors. God renews us to make us useful for Kingdom work. Allow God to do a new thing in you and through you.

Are you consuming new or old wine? Are you a new or old wineskin?

Verses:

Matthew 9:16-17

Mark 2:21-22

Luke 5:36-39-

Genesis 49:11

Proverbs 20:1

Jeremiah 31:29

Ezekiel 18:1-4

Challenge:

Ask God to show you if you have any ritualistic religious practices that you need to let go. List them and pray to ensure they are not idols in your life. These rituals should never be placed with as high a priority in our life as having a genuine relationship with Our Savior and each other. These belong to an old paradigm that Jesus resurrected from, for us to shift away and break through. As a bonus compare the passages in Matthew, Mark and Luke. Note how they are similar or different.

Prayer:

Dad, thank You for allowing me to see any religious practices that I have idolized. Help me to be renewed and transformed by Your Word and Your presence. Help me to cast down all my idols and worship You in spirit and in truth. I love You! Amen!

My Notes

Seedless Fruit

I've heard many brothers and sisters say they feel off because they missed a week of church. In general, they have a weekly testimony that they barely have enough strength to make it into, "God's House, one more time." Do you run from church conference to church conference? Do you know all the preachers who can preach—Preach preacher!— and listen to one pastor after another? Do you find yourself constantly searching for the next good word, while constantly playing one message after the other?

If so, you may need to check the fruit that you ingest. None of these actions are bad in moderation, but as we mature, we must get The Word from the source. We have to stop expecting someone to regurgitate a predigested portion of The Word for us, when we have teeth to chew for ourselves. We are told to taste and see that the Lord is good. We shouldn't want someone to pre-taste for us. We must go to the Vine if we want to get the message that will sustain us. We shouldn't be satisfied with a temporary fill of a processed meal. We need the life sustaining Word. It will give us more than enough with more to share with others, turning them into disciples, too.

We are called to bear fruit. When the process is organic, there will be a potent seed in it. If not, we will just create a mutation of ourselves. We will produce good fruit while connected to the True Vine. The seed in it will not only nourish others, but also it will give them the ability to produce an abundant harvest and replicate the same process. When you show others how to be Christlike, and not just a replica of you, your church, or your denomination, then the Earth can be like Heaven.

Verses:

Genesis 1:11-12

Isaiah 11:1

Isaiah 27:6

Galatians 5:22-23

Psalm 92:12-15

Proverbs 11:30

Proverbs 18:21

Challenge:

Read the full chapters for the verses in this week's devotional. Find a way to share the Good News revealed to you in at least one of these chapters with someone this week. It doesn't have to be a sermon. Ask God for the opportunity and the appropriate testimony.

Prayer:

Lord, please mature me so I can produce the fruit of the Spirit according to Galatians 5:22-23. Let me bear love, joy, peace, patience, goodness, faithfulness, gentleness, humility, and self-control in abundance through my connection with You. As I connect with others, please allow the same fruit to manifest in their lives—multiplying on Earth what already abounds in Heaven. Amen!

My Notes

Damaged Plant = Bad Fruit

My tomato plants were growing well, until one of the summer's many storms hit. The plants laid over and looked like they were going to die. I went to purchase a tomato cage, and with help I placed it around the plants. The cage provides boundary and support to the tomato plant as it begins to grow. As I placed the cage around the plants, I heard a crunching sound that didn't sound too good. I knew I had to continue, because by that point I realized why the cage was important for the plant.

Weeks later, some of the leaves started to die. I realized either I had damaged one of the plants, or either the plant had gotten sick. The plants both continued to grow, mostly healthy and pretty strong. I started to figure the plant must be pretty resilient. Maybe the crunching sound that I heard didn't affect the plant that much. I started to see the flowers, and then small tomato babies! I was super excited.

Then as the tomatoes continued to grow and develop, I saw the truth. The plant was indeed sick or damaged. Even though most of the leaves appeared to be healthy, and the fruit had started to grow. The evidence was very clear in the fruit that rotted before it could fully develop. I was upset as I took my first few half-brown tomatoes off and threw them away. I thought because the flowers had bloomed, and the fruit began to grow, that the damage had repaired itself, but I wasn't right. At this point I wanted to throw the whole plant away, but I had more than one tomato plant in the same container. I didn't want to damage or risk pulling up the wrong plant, so I left both plants to grow together.

One plant had a few larger tomatoes that were starting to ripen, and I was very excited by it. The other produced only the small sick fruit, which made me disappointed every time I had to remove the tomatoes just to throw them out. Maybe I should have handled it differently, but I was still learning, and I was also hopeful that my sick and damaged plant would heal and produce good fruit.

At times, I've noticed that my fruit has been bad. It was plainly spoken to me that I had unforgiveness in my roots. When that happened, I ask God to heal, fix, repair, and remove me from this wild vine and to please graft me back in with the True Vine. I don't know why I am always surprised that there could be bad fruit. I am always thrown off by the experience. I'm continuously thinking about how it is such a feat to mature and produce fruit. Never realizing that, yes, I can still produce death, if I'm not grounded right.

Although I've heard God referred to as the True Vine, I don't think I realized that there is a false vine that produces bad grapes and bad wine. There is always a decoy available, it looks like this:

"For their vine is from the vine of Sodom, And from the fields of Gomorrah; Their grapes are grapes of poison, Their clusters, bitter. Their wine is the venom of serpents, And the deadly poison of cobras." (Deuteronomy 32:32-33, NASB)

We are also taught there can be bad fruit. I guess that is why we are told we can recognize the false by its fruit. For a time, people can masquerade and call themselves Christians, but through storms, growth, and maturity it becomes very apparent when there is something else in the mix.

Our Healer has the capable hand to heal us when we have been hurt and damaged by life. Sometimes we think, *I'm over that; it doesn't even bother me anymore.* The problem is that it may be a deeper scar than we are able to discern, and it may not be apparent to us that we are producing rotten fruit. It takes many fruit-bearing trees several years before they produce fruit. I thought it was the end state to produce fruit. I was recently reminded that these trees take several more years and many additional seasons to mature and produce fruit that can also be sweet and fit for consumption. Allow God to determine what is healed and what still needs to be touched by Him. God can fix or remove the root issues.

Verses:

Matthew 7:15-20

Matthew 10:1

Matthew 12:33

Luke 3:9

Luke 13:11-13

Acts 10:38

James 5:14-16

Challenge:

Ask God to reveal to you the areas that need healing, for you to bear good fruit in the Kingdom. It has been revealed to me that I've struggled with unforgiveness on numerous occasions. Feel free to write down your area(s) and any healing experiences that you've had. As a bonus, look up the Rose of Jericho and see what spiritual lessons are revealed to you by this plant's lifecycle.

Prayer:

God, I submit my whole body to You to use for Your Will and service for Your Kingdom. Take my life God, allow me to work with You to expand the Kingdom. Allow my fruit to be nourishing and healing for others. Also, please allow my situations and testimonies to shed light in this world. I want my fruit to be good, just like You created it to be. Please heal me so I can heal others. Please help me to show the love, grace and mercy that You have shown to me. I love You! Amen!

My Notes

WEEK 31

Gardening With
the Master Gardener

Several years ago, my sons and I started a small container farm on the back porch. We had a variety of plants and seedlings. Some started from seeds, some from food scraps, and some were baby plants from a local store. God used this to show me about His Kingdom. No matter how we got into His garden, He has selected us and cared for us because we are now His. He has paid the price and made sacrifice to have us with Him. He provides what is necessary to grow His plants, seeds, and even the scraps that others would just throw away, into mature plants that will bear much fruit.

However, we must experience dirt, rain, and heat for our development. God knows we will go through messy situations. Sometimes they are caused by poor decisions—all are designed for us to overcome. He will cause the rain to come on us. We should take it in as refreshing and cleansing, while striving to see the silver lining in the clouds. Sometimes the heat is turned up in our lives. Do we enjoy the warmth, or do we break out in a sweat and become more miserable as the degrees increase?

It was brought to my attention that I wanted to shield my sons, my seed, from anything negative in this world. I had the desire for them to never be hurt, uncomfortable, scared, disappointed, or any of the other perceived negative emotions. But that does not allow them to grow in a functional way. What we call the good, the bad, and the ugly are just a part of life.

While my oldest son was studying abroad in China for a third semester, he started to experience difficulties. He had struggles with some of his classes, growth, maturity, and he was experiencing spiritual warfare. I prayed for him and sent out prayer requests when I was made aware of the situations. A big part of me wanted him to come home where I could watch over him. God continually assured me the He was always with both of us and would never leave. I also recognized the opportunity for him to use some of his gifts. This was just basic training. Warriors must be trained. I reminded him that part of his mission is to reunite The Kingdom. My son has been entrusted with the gift to interpret tongues. He was in the perfect environment to continue to sharpen his skills while living in an international dorm in a foreign land.

I am sure we are also in the perfect environment for our growth, development, and maturation.

Verses:

Matthew 5:44-45

Ecclesiastes 9:11

Jeremiah 12:1-3

Luke 8:5-15

2 Corinthians 9:6-15

Romans 5:2

1 Thessalonians 5:18

Challenge:

Identify areas in your life where you either feel as though the heat has been turned up or there's a gray cloud threatening a downpour. Ask God to help you see the tough times in your life as beneficial for your growth and development. Walk in the revelation that these experiences are helping establish you as more than a conqueror. You are victorious!

Prayer:

God, thank You for ensuring my proper growth and development. Please allow me to see the benefits of the situations in which I find myself. Allow me to be grateful for the opportunity to bear much fruit for the Kingdom. Amen!

My Notes

WEEK 32

The Pollinator

I had no idea my garden would have flowers in it. After all, I planted a vegetable and herb garden. I am beginning to see small flowers develop on some of my pea, green bean, tomato, and basil plants. A flower signifies that the plant has matured. This is not the final state for the plant, it is a signal that a new season has begun. It also serves to attract the pollinator which will allow the plant to serve its purpose of bearing fruit.

Depending on the fruit, it may be pollinated in one or more ways, including wind and insect pollination. But the plant isn't changed into the pollinator. No, the pollinator comes to make the plant a much more productive version of itself. This leads me to understand more about the Body. We need interactions with people who may not be part of our church house to help us to bear fruit. Be sure these interactions don't change you into the world, but they should transform the world into the image of God. This pollination process leads to many being satisfied. It also allows the process to replicate itself on grander scales each time. I heard once that each apple has a whole orchard in it. Each Christian has the Kingdom in him or her! Don't just go to church and go home. Don't just study to show yourself that you are approved. Be fruitful, flower, and multiply!

I think this is the very reason Jesus spent so much time with the undesirables of His time. He is our perfect example of how we are to live. If we were supposed to only associate with our sisters and brothers from our local church, we would see Jesus only hanging out with folk from His local church. I don't see that in the Bible, so it leads me to live my life in a much more open sense. In this way, He allows me to learn about Him from varying points of view. He allows me to see holes in the religion that I had been practicing. He shows me how to grow more into the image of Our Father.

It is a relief as well. Sometimes I don't feel like I fit in with the more churched folk. I like jeans and tennis shoes. I couldn't tell you exactly how or when to praise. I don't know how to cut the right step or how to give the best shout. And I don't have the best Christian phrase to apply in every situation. I do know that God is real! He desires to have a relationship with me, and He finds me valuable, even in my imperfect state.

In that particular season, God revealed to me that I was a pollinator. I should be open to go to various locations on Sunday or other days, as I am led. I have to be willing to receive or give The Word wherever I am. I spread events to the people who I know may benefit from them, whether they attend my church or not; I just pass on the resources as it seems appropriate. I am willing to listen to other pastors, read devotionals, and books, as led. We need to break down the silos in the church, so we can truly be one Body.

Verses:

Isaiah 35:1-2

Isaiah 40:6-8

Luke 12:27

Song of Solomon 2:11-12

1 Peter 1:23-25

Psalm 103:15-16

James 1:27

Challenge:

Be willing to step outside of your comfort zone. Listen and let God lead you to visit someplace outside of church to be the Church, being aware of the fact that the Kingdom is on the inside of you. Take someone with you or at least share what you learned with someone else.

Prayer:

Thank You, God, for allowing the visible to show us more about what is usually invisible to us. Thank You for sending me where I am needed to advance Your Kingdom. Please allow me to be sensitive to the Spirit and maintain a willing spirit. Allow the perfect mixing so that Your Kingdom will come and Your perfect Will is done here on Earth as it is in Heaven. Amen!

My Notes

WEEK 33

Take Inventory

I had only two tomatoes from my plant when I became hooked. I was convinced that these were the best tomatoes I had ever tasted. I shared them within my own house, but I didn't produce a large enough harvest to share like I really wanted. After that, I spent a lot of time watching and nurturing the plant. Once I had about nine tomatoes I could think about sharing. I wanted others to be able to experience this for themselves and not just merely hear about my experience. I thought I could give them a tomato, soil, and a mini pot. Hopefully, they would decide like I have, that this will be a lifestyle. I plan to grow tomatoes every year from here on out!

When I heard God tell me to do an inventory, I started thinking of some emergency supplies I had shelved in the back room. This morning, I understood more clearly as He told me its spiritual and encouraged me to take inventory of my fruit.

"But the fruit of the Spirit is love, joy, peace, patience, kindness, goodness, faithfulness, gentleness, and self-control. Against such things there is no law." (Galatians 5:22–23, Berean Study Bible)

I have each of the components, He ensured that! However, have I done the work for there to be an increase? Do I desire to only have enough self-control to just not go off and give people a piece of my mind in a negative situation? Do I want just enough peace to be still around me, or do I want to bring and deposit peace in the room?

Abundant living is realized when the excess doesn't just overflow and get wasted. It allows others to be bathed in the overflow from God that is flowing through you. Does your fruit have a potent seed you can leave with someone, or is it just enough to feed yourself? As I take inventory of the fruit of the Spirit, I realize that it is not enough to have the fruit for show, but I have to have a real abundance to share. I am about to check on my fruit, first, to see where He leads me next.

Verses:

Daniel 4 :12

Ezekiel 17 :8

James 3:17-18

Romans 12:3

Galatians 5:1, 22-23

Titus 3:4-5

2 Samuel 2:6

Challenge:

Reread the verses about the fruit of the Spirit and take a spiritual inventory. Is it enough to sustain you through life's circumstances? What do you have in abundance that's stored up in case of emergencies? Did you find yourself running short on anything during the pandemic in 2020? Do you have enough to share with family, loved ones, the nation, and/or the world?

Prayer:

Lord, please allow us to mature what You've placed in us as a seed. As we become fruitful, let us think of others who are less fortunate than us in the area(s) You have given us abundance. Let us use the overflow for the advancement of Your Kingdom, in Jesus' Name. Amen!

My Notes

WEEK 34

Agape: Love Personified

I had to do some looking around to understand what is meant by the statement that Christians are to love. We are told to Love God, Love our neighbor, and even to Love our enemy.

I grew up influenced heavily by *Disney* and my imagination. I had a happily-ever-after fantasy of love. The mushy, feeling butterflies in your stomach, kind of love. But we are not called to just have a feeling.

Jesus showed us how to be Love. He modeled it for us every day and in every story written about Him. I think the main difference is when you Love (verb) you give yourself permission to allow that love to change, or your actions to change or stop. When I am Love (noun) I don't have permission to change or stop being. I am a mom, I am a Christian, I am a child of God, I am Love. It is the very character of who I am.

In churches that equip for discipleship, we are taught to love God, our neighbors, and enemies. But we may not be taught that it is our very nature to be Love, simply by being a child of God. So, as we try to mature, we struggle to perform the beatitudes in Matthew like it is a checklist. However, it is simply explaining to us what it looks like when we simply become what we are created to be, His Love. He wants us to be Love, and not just look like or pretend to do it.

They will know we are Christians by our Love. But do they know? Can they discern the difference between professing Christians and the world? Can we even tell the difference? Are we willing to be the difference?

Verses:

Ephesians 4:1-6

John 13:34-35

Matthew 5:43-46

Mathew 24:12

Luke 6:27-36

Genesis 29:18-20

Proverbs 17:17

Challenge:

Look up the definition for, love, as a verb and noun. Note how they are similar yet different. Think about opportunities that you passed up in the past week to be Love. Be mindful to take the opportunities as they present themselves in the upcoming week.

Prayer:

Thank You for loving and being Love to us in the most perfect way. Allow us to just be what You created us to be before the foundations of the Earth. Let my, "I love You," extend to my neighbor and even my enemies.
Amen!

My Notes

WEEK 35

Inheritance 101

In Genesis 2:16-17, the Lord God commanded the man saying, "From any tree of the garden you may eat freely; but from the tree of the knowledge of good and evil you shall not eat, for in the day that you eat from it you will surely die."

The death experienced by Adam was while he was still in the land of the living.

I was told by God to share the following with someone who has a deep knowledge of insurance and insurance policies. I asked him how my beneficiaries get paid off from my life insurance policy after I've passed away. I was told once my death had been verified, the insurance company pays the predetermined percentage of the inheritance to each beneficiary. I asked, what happens if someone doesn't feel the beneficiary is worthy? I also asked, what happens if the beneficiary doesn't feel they deserve the inheritance? In both cases, the inheritance is delivered to the beneficiary/beneficiaries without a determination of whether they deserve the inheritance or not.

The point is this, Jesus died on the cross to give us an inheritance, now. Everlasting Life starts, now. Heaven starts, now. The Kingdom is at hand. Everlasting or eternal means it has no end and no beginning. It means bookend to bookend. The blood is retroactive and last through eternity. He has already defeated death, Hell, and the grave. What are you going to do with your inheritance?

Verses:

2 Timothy 1:9

John 5:24

1 Peter 1:3-5

Psalm 28:9

Ephesians 1:18

Romans 8:16-18

Isaiah 43:10-13

Challenge:

Read 1 Peter, Chapter 1. List actions from your past that have made you feel unworthy or unjustified of your rightful inheritance. Rip up the list, remembering, "It is finished!"

Prayer:

God, thank You for providing the sacrifice to fully atone for the penalty of sin. I trust You and I believe You, alone, have made me worthy of this inheritance. Help me to show others this truth. I love You! Amen!

My Notes

The Ultimate Example of Humility: Jesus — A Real-down-to-Earth Kind of God

In the beginning, God created us in His very likeness. We were deceived into believing we needed something else to be like God. So, we had to taste the fruit of the knowledge of good and evil. We, mankind, seemed to believe that God was God only because He had some forbidden knowledge and we needed that to be like Him.

Then we desired and He gave us a list of laws to follow. I believe those laws were to show us what we were created to be. They were less of a checklist and more of a mirror to show us who we are. I naturally don't have a desire to break most of the laws. I don't have to strive, every day, not to steal, kill, and destroy. I'm not saying, I've never had a bad thought. But that just isn't my normal demeanor.

However, we still didn't understand what God created, and we tried to keep hundreds of rules and laws but found the task daunting. We lived under the assumption that no one could keep all of those laws that we were trying to keep. So, we then used holy men to stand in the gap for us. We had them make sacrifices to atone for our sins on a regular basis.

I believe God came to Earth as Jesus to show us exactly what we were created to be in the beginning, just like Him and a part of Him. Jesus didn't use His deity. He came as humbly as He could. He was born in a manger. Who can say they were born that meagerly? He rode into town on a donkey. My ride is slightly nicer and less smelly! He was showing us that the less we try in our own strength, the more we just are His creation. We are able to do all the things He designed us to do. Why? Because He is the Master Creator!

Have you ever seen a car trying to be a car, a bird trying to be a bird, or a house trying to be a house? I don't even have to try to be Diane and Charles' daughter, I just am, and it is obvious. You are a child of God, you just are, nothing to prove, nothing to try. Just be it! He guides and matures us; we just have to be willing. Now that God has showed us it is possible, please don't let Jesus be the last example of humility. Let's not be discouraged, but let's use our humble beginnings as a testimony to someone else on the journey. If you get this lesson, pass it on. If not, pray until you get the clear revelation of who He created you to be—His own!

Verses:

Genesis 1:26-27

Genesis 3:4-6

Luke 2:7

Leviticus 14:19

Matthew 21:1-5

John 1:12-13

1 John 3:1-2

Challenge:

Look up, read, write, and memorize all 613 Levitical laws. Or simply thank God for the sacrifice of Jesus Christ, Who fulfilled the whole law. The choice is yours!

Prayer:

Thank You for showing us that we shouldn't despise humble beginnings. Please teach us that there is strength in humility. Amen!

My Notes

I Got the Keys to the Condo
and the Kingdom

One year, even though I was on a budget, I was very fortunate to be able to travel multiple times. I went to Pennsylvania, but only had to pay for one of the nights in the hotel. I stayed with friends in Atlanta and New York for free. My most recent trip was to the beach. My friend's family has a timeshare, and they were generous enough to allow me and my kids to stay, again for free!

My surrogate brother granted me permission and simply dropped off the keys. He didn't give me a rundown of rules or restrictions. He just gave me the keys and told me to enjoy. I accepted the offer and used the keys to enter the condo, day after day, during my wonderful vacation.

As Christians, we have been given keys to the Kingdom through Jesus and His sacrifice. He has shown us how to get home. As a Thank You, we can, and should, show others how to get into the Kingdom as well. We are to follow Jesus' example of unconditional love, relationship, obedience, and many other qualities that were placed in us from the beginning. Don't just hold your keys and not use them! Allow someone else to follow your example as you follow Jesus back home to the Father's House.

He has given us the keys needed to set the captives free. He even has the keys to Hell, or have you forgotten? Will you use them for freedom, or will you continue to feel that you or others are unworthy?

Verses:

Isaiah 22:22

Matthew 16:19

Matthew 23:13

Revelation 1:18

Luke 11:52

Acts 14:22

Psalm 49:13-15

Challenge:

Show someone the way home, but without a list of rules or an invitation to your local church. Introduce them to the Way, the Truth, and the Life through your actions.

Prayer:

*God, thank You for coming as Jesus and showing me the
Way, the Truth and the Life! Please use me as a living
sacrifice. Let my life be the light to illuminate the path for
someone else. Show me how to effectively use the keys
You have given me. Allow me to be active, powerful,
and giving. Give me the opportunity to show people how
to have a relationship with You. I love You! Amen!*

My Notes

Cleared for Flight — Wheels Up!

In a dream, we were waiting for the flight to take off. But the airplane had to go down a street that seemed like the Washington, D.C. metropolitan Beltway, to get to the runway. We were sitting in traffic and we could see traffic on the other side of the road, too. I thought it was strange, but it seemed normal for this airline to have to drive on the street until it could take off. We had to keep our seats straight in the upright position, the seat was hurting some people's necks because the top made their heads tip forward. We received water bottles from the flight attendants. I wrapped mine in a sheet and placed it behind my neck. It relieved the pressure and opened up my chest some, causing me to feel more comfortable.

While we were waiting, everyone's attention was on a bad accident on the other side of the street. However, I later realized these cars were manufactured without roofs and placed on the highway to look like there had been an accident. Although it appeared to be a multi-car pileup, the drama was created just to be a distraction, there was no real accident!

There is supposed to be drama, accidents, and incidents on the road; especially, if it is leading away from God. In my dream, I don't think there were any accidents on my side of the road either, just rubbernecking looking at what the rest of the world was doing. In real life, I'm supposed to be flying! I've been sitting waiting for things to clear up, when I should already be high above the traffic and certainly not worried about accidents on the other side of the street. Please reveal to me how to correct this, Father, and how to keep my eyes on You at all times!

Verses:

Hebrews 2:1-4

Ecclesiastes 11:1-6

1 Samuel 10:6-7

Revelation 14:6-7

Isaiah 6:1-3

Psalm 55:6-8

Isaiah 40:31

Challenge:

Take a week off from the news, newspaper, or social media newsfeeds, and allow the Good News to take that time slot. Write down any noteworthy revelations you receive during this time. There will be plenty of bad news around after the week is over if you choose to indulge again. As a bonus, read and compare 2 Samuel 22 and Psalm 18.

Prayer:

Please, God, help me to remember that I was designed to fly, and distractions were designed to distract. Please help me to stay on course and follow Your Will. I love You.
Amen!

My Notes

WEEK 39

America, the Glutton

We have probably all experienced at least some of these things:

You can never have enough: handbags, shoes, clothes, coats, etc.

Stock up and save

Big box stores

Fast-food

Super-size

All you can eat

5XL

Gonna get my blessings

Increase, increase, lose your mind for increase! (That's what a once popular gospel song encouraged us to do.)

McMansions

Storage units

Maxed-out social media friends/followers list

Show binge watching

What do all of these things have in common? Excess! Gluttony means greedy or excessive indulgence. We live in a society where too much isn't enough. Look at the landscape, it screams, "You need more, and you need it now!"

Oh, you want a small 24-ounce soda?? Sure! But why not upsize for twenty-five cents more!?

Why not just get a case of it for just a little more?

You need some place to live, why not get a ten-bedroom house?

You don't have too much stuff; you just need a place to store more!

More, more, more and it's never enough! God blesses, and we still look for more. When are we going to be satisfied?

According to my BMI and doctor, I'm obese. I was very okay with this common diagnosis. I stopped growing vertically around twenty-five years ago, horizontally not so much. I decided to walk and eat healthier—a normal prescription. But it's so hard to exercise off overindulgence! The more often I exercised, the more often I felt hungry.

God recently directed me to fast, and I instantly got sad. Before this week, I really had a negative reaction to just the thought of turning my plate down. Don't get me wrong, I have experienced some of the best times with God and can always hear Him so clearly when I fast. But I loved food, I was addicted, I never had enough. Even when I was full, I was plotting the next meal. How could I not? I have growing sons who are always hungry. If they are hungry, I must be at least a little hungry. I would at least snack while they ate. With all the good stuff I'm seeing and smelling, why deny myself? We are so afraid of starving to death that we will gladly eat ourselves to death.

In just a few days, I was clearly able to see my addiction and I started taking the steps to correct this, including prayer. I had to stop pretending that my body still had these incredible demands for calories. I had to realize that I had been conditioned to eat three to five times, if not constantly, during the day. But if anyone or scripture had the nerve to insinuate that I should commune with Our Father that often, I thought they were doing too much, and that it was not possible. This is not a suggested diet plan. I'm hopeful to change a mindset.

What has society conformed and confused your mind to think excess is a necessity? What do you spend more time doing than being with God and being like Jesus for everyone to see? Take it to God, so you can ensure that this isn't an idol-god for you. Make sure nothing is rivaling the place only God should hold, which is #1!

In America, we have a different food to celebrate for every day of the year. What do you think would happen if Christians decided to celebrate and embody the fruit of the Spirit every day? Would we look differently?! Would America? Would the world?

Verses:

Ephesians 5:3

Matthew 17:21* (specifically look at NIV, 1984)

Mark 9:29

Haggai 1:6-7

2 Peter 1:2-4

Proverbs 23:20-21

Philippians 3:18-19

Challenge:

Take note to see if the translation(s) you read includes directions to fast with prayer. Identify an area of excess in your life. Commit to unplug from whatever God revealed to you for the next week. Spend that additional time reading, pondering, and sharing The Word.

Prayer:

God, please allow our minds, that have previously been conformed to this world, to be transformed and freed by this revealed truth. In Jesus' Name. Amen!

My Notes

I Swear or Firmly Attest to Believe the Truth, the Whole Truth, and Nothing but the Truth

I have been sick and unable to eat for a week. I've been eating small, mostly vegetarian meals, once a day, but even that seems to be hard for my stomach to digest. I tried to give myself a digestive enzyme. That was a big mistake! I still didn't digest the chicken breast, that I insisted on eating, or anything else. I also had an anaphylaxis-type of extreme adverse reaction to the papaya enzyme. My body ordered that nothing more was coming in, and everything that was in me must come out.

The next day I was filled with lies. One was about my medical condition and suggested course of action. The doctor prescribed heartburn medicine and a trip to the allergist. The allergist really listened and informed me that my reaction was not an allergy; and many of the reactions I had attributed to allergies were in fact, not. He suggested I see a Gastroenterologist (GI) specialist for my digestion problems. However, my primary care doctor was not on board. She only wanted me to take the prescribed medicine, although it was opposite of what I needed for my condition and symptoms. She didn't want me to have a referral to the GI specialist, unless I didn't feel better for an additional two-to-four weeks. She also misrepresented the truth about my appointment with her. She lied about what she had told me during our visit a few hours prior. I stood up for myself and got the referral. I also set her straight, or at least gave her a piece of my mind.

The only bit of truth she slipped in was when she said, "Sometimes us doctors do too much, the body can heal itself if we just give it time."

I have been self-medicating for more than twenty years and have only had this one bad reaction. I wish I could say the same about my experience with the medical profession. My children and I have had many misdiagnoses, mistreatments, and overdoses while under a doctor's care. I've wrecked my digestive system and had other adverse reactions, while believing the truths of one physician or another.

I went back to the supplement store to return the enzyme, received good advice, and a wonderful coconut kefir probiotic! I went with my track record and trusted what has worked in my past almost every time. Don't quit your doctor! A few are good and believe in what they do. They can also see your blood, cells, and many things you cannot, when they actually look, listen, and feel. I get along with my current doctor much better. She told me, "God sends them, and I just listen." I appreciate that. I'm not giving medical advice, it's spiritual.

What truth have you substituted for God's Truth? God can do more than run a few scans and do choice tests. He can diagnose and fully heal the problem whether it is spiritual, emotional, or physical. He can test the heart and our motives. We can't esteem anything or anybody to God's place. We can trust Him and His perfect track record. God never fails!

Verses:

Romans 1:25

John 8:31-32

Deuteronomy 32:3-4

Psalm 31:1-5

Isaiah 65:16

2 Corinthians 1:20-22

John 17:13-21

Challenge:

Ask God to test your motives against the plumb line of Truth. Allow Him to show you the areas that you can work on and the areas where you need to yield and trust Him to fully fix.

Prayer:

God, I thank You for being more than just a good doctor, but for being the Master Surgeon. Today, I yield myself to Your Almighty hand. Please reveal, reprove, and reprise me as You see fit. I love You. Amen!

My Notes

WEEK 41

Software Upgrade

As I was getting ready for bed, one evening, I realized that my phone was on less than fifty percent and my charger was in the car. There was no way that I was leaving the house to get the charger, but I was concerned. I had an older iPhone which can go from fifty to zero percent, quickly. I had an important meeting, where I was standing in for my client and lead in the morning, so I had to make sure I was awake and on time. There was a phone charger in the kitchen, but I had not been able to successfully use it for the past couple of weeks. I plugged the phone in, it signaled it was charging right away, *Thank You, Jesus!*

But then I noticed it had been plugged in for a while and the battery percentage was not increasing. I had a nightly prayer on the phone with my mom and afterward the battery percentage was still the same. I read the verse of the day online, and I noticed the percentage was lower. *Really!* was my thought, *It's plugged in!* I unplugged and re-plugged the phone. Then the battery percentage started to slowly creep up. I had to unplug and re-plug the phone several times overnight. In the morning, it was finally at ninety-three percent. I woke up to a message on my screen that software update was not completed because my phone was not connected to the power source between 2 to 5 a.m.

Most of us spend six or more hours, each night, resting or attempting to rest. Personally, I need at least eight hours. Do we spend that time idle, allowing our mind to roam wherever it wishes? Or are we intentionally dedicating that time to God, allowing us to hear His revelations, letting our mind go where He sends it, and just spending that time with the lover of our souls? In my dreams, I am often with many people. Recently, I have had a few vivid dreams in which I am interceding for others in prayer and spiritual warfare, providing a safe place in times of trouble, keeping gates, and praising and worshipping God fervently and loudly.

For the past year, before I go to bed, I pray in part, that God will allow me to spend time with Him in the Secret Place or that He sends me where I am needed. Connect to the power source, not only in the day, but also at night. Commit your rest to Him and see what changes you notice in your relationship and in your effectiveness. Allow Him to upgrade your software! Sharing the secrets of the Kingdom and the desires of His heart as you rest. Take notice as you are more prepared for your personal life challenges and to be a blessing to others despite your challenges.

Verses:

Romans 12:2

Proverbs 3:24-26

Proverbs 6:22

Psalm 3:5

Colossians 2:19

Psalm 71:7

Psalm 18:30-35 (TPT specifically)

Challenge:

Purposely unplug from the T.V. or social media before bed. Pray before you go to bed and spend some time with God. Ask Him to direct your path even as you sleep.

Prayer:

Dear Heavenly Father, thank You for the revelations You give us in the night season. Thank You for the ability to be able to connect to the true power source even as we rest. Amen!

My Notes

WEEK 42

The Gatekeeper

I had a dream I was at my parents' house. When I went in, there was a baby gate at the top of their staircase. They were hosting some type of get-together and there were children in the bedrooms down the hall. I was standing at the top of the steps in the hallway, when a very well-mannered and soft-spoken older lady was coming up the stairs. She nicely asked me to move the gate. But somehow, I knew she was up to no good and I kept telling her, "no." She kept trying to convince me to move the gate to let her come further into the bedroom area. She even tried to move it herself, but for some reason, she was not able.

A little later, my dad was coming up the steps. He moved the gate as he reached the top of the stairs. I am not sure he really noticed or acknowledged the lady. At this time, I had two large kitchen knives in my hands and had to rush to place the gate in the hallway, so she couldn't get to the bedrooms. I kept yelling at her as she asked me to move the gate. I shouted, "I'm a gate keeper and I'll keep on guarding the gate!" Not familiar at all with the concept, I had to look it up.

Verses:

2 Samuel 18:24-27

1 Chronicles 9:23-24

2 Chronicles 8:14

2 Chronicles 23:4-7

Nehemiah 7:1-2

Nehemiah 10:28-30

Nehemiah 13:22

Challenge:

Read more about gatekeepers in the Bible, specifically as depicted in Nehemiah. Do we have a need for present-day gatekeepers? If so, who are they or who should they be?

Prayer:

God, please continue to reveal things to me about You, Your Word, myself, and whatever You would like. Please use my sleep time for Your glory while I get sweet rest. Amen!

My Notes

WEEK 43

San Francisco — Connect the Dots

I had a dream that a lady with whom I used to attend church, lived across the street from me. This dream was in the house from the series *Full House*, that I watched growing up. This episode looked like it was from the first season, because baby Michelle was there. Both of the Olsen twins, who played baby Michelle, were being held by someone sitting in the kitchen. As I looked out of my window to see MH put her children on the school bus, I kept thinking I didn't know she lived on my street, Francisco Court.

When I woke up, I sent MH a text to let her know she once again had cameoed in my dream. Then, I remembered the show took place in San Francisco, and I sent her that message too. She texted back that she had just dreamt of a lady she knew who had recently moved to San Francisco.

I looked up the meaning of Francisco and I read that it meant *free man*. There was also a mention of Saint Francis, a saint who took a vow of poverty and spent most of his life rebuilding the church.

She then sent me a video she came across on Facebook from Pastor Francis Chan, titled *Is God pleased with our churches?* "Please take a look at it, if you have time," was her message.

A couple days later, my son was looking for a Bible on *Biblegateway.com* and there was an advertisement to sign up for two of Pastor Francis Chan's Devotional Series: *Crazy Love* and *Relentless God*. Of course, I signed up, immediately, and I let MH know about it also. That Monday, I received the *Crazy Love* devotional and found out it was the very first day of the devotional series. The message reminded me to not only pray to God, but also to ensure I listen as well.

What I receive in response may or may not be a solution or an answer to what I prayed. There may be something completely separate on the heart of God in that moment or season. I then listened to the video, Pastor Francis Chan mentioned in the devotional, and then another, on the third video he was addressing a group in San Francisco, where I later found out he lived. When I shared this story with another friend, Kym, she told me she just got back from a trip to San Francisco.

What's the point?! I am not so sure. I just wanted to show you how God speaks and leads me. Sometimes I get it, sometimes I just don't. I do know He has been relentless in His pursuit of me and He is very deliberate in ensuring that I understand my value and purpose. It's just a part of my love journey with Our Father, and I am just sharing it with you.

Verses:

John 13:7

Psalm 37:23

Psalm 119:133

Proverbs 2:6-9

Jeremiah 40:4

1 Peter 2:16

Romans 6:22

Challenge:

In the next week, take note of connections, synchronicity, and common themes; and trust the process!

Prayer:

Lord, please help us to trust You fully as You lead us and guide us on the path of righteousness. Please cover and protect everyone in San Francisco. Allow Your ministering angels to speak Your Word to this region. If anyone does not know You, please let them encounter You in a way that will leave them forever marked by You. Please show Your Love, grace, and mercy to San Francisco, and all the people who call it home. In Jesus' Name. Amen!

My Notes

Prayer Power — A Poem

What is the Body using the power of prayer to petition Heaven for? Is it for self or for others? When I hear from Heaven are there selfless or selfish request? Do I hear Thank You or complaints about how the blessing could have been better? Do I hear praise or pitiful pleas for me, mine, more, and my way? Do you use the scriptures for My Will, to advance The Kingdom, and to show forth My Glory on the Earth as it is in Heaven? Or is it for witchcraft, for your disobedience, and to paint the perfect portrait as far as your short sightedness can see it?

When I do work through you, do you steal My shine,

or give me the glory and honor that you know should be Mine?

Others have a need and I've given you the provision.

What do you say? "God will make a way.

He will assist you on your mission."

What role did I give you?

Will you walk past while your brother goes through?

Turn a blind eye, wonder why,

say a prayer and not be there.

They are worth everything to Me.

Clean out your eyes so you can see.

I have made everyone My treasure.

I love you all beyond measure.

Give up your emergency-room bed for someone who is actually sick.

Stop lying around unarmored, and unprepared for the enemy's next trick.

Turn from you, and back to Me.

From yourself, and sin, you must flee.

I conquered death, Hell, and the grave.

I gave My life, so you may save.

Use the freedom given to you to free.

Stop making your religion about *me, me, me*.

Then I will hear from Heaven and heal your land.

I am here, leading, and guiding,

When will you take My hand?

Verses:

2 Chronicles 7:14-16

1 Kings 8:30

Deuteronomy 9:25-27

Numbers 11:1-2

Numbers 14:26-28

Proverbs 15:8

Matthew 6:5-13

Challenge:

Find someone to pray for. There are so many sick, bereaved, and hurting people. Intercede and petition the Father on that person's behalf, just as someone has done for you.

Prayer:

The Lord's Prayer

Our Father Who is in Heaven,

Hallowed be Your name.

Your Kingdom come.

Your will be done,

on earth as it is in heaven.

Give us this day our daily bread.

And forgive us our debts, as we also have forgiven our debtors.

And do not lead us into temptation,

but deliver us from evil.

For Yours is the Kingdom

and the power and the glory forever.

Amen. (Matthew 6:9(b)-13, NASB)

My Notes

A Man After God's Own
Heart—A Jagged Pill

The 2016 election had done more than reveal what is in the heart of the country. It revealed the cancer in the church. It exposed what had been swept under a rug and not dealt with. Some card-carrying Christians haven't spoken to God in a very long time. Not only are we not speaking to God, but also, we aren't listening either. Many present a wish list and a box in which God must remain in for us to let Him be our God. This foolishness must stop! We have to start practicing what we preach. If we can make up quotes and misquote the scripture to suit our own agenda, then it's time to start living in *truth*.

If *God is good all the time, and, all the time, God is good*, then why do we think this situation is bad, very bad. Why are we sad, very sad? Why is it okay for us to believe that nearly half of the country is bigoted, but once it hits fifty percent then, *God help us*? So, it would have been fine, if fifty million people wanted Trump and spewed hate, as long as Hillary was our President? Why are we hollering, "Jesus take the wheel!" when He should already have it—if we are who we claim to be.

I think the 2016 election was also the whatever-it-takes catalyst to wake up the Church, the Body, and the Bride. If you can't wake up with joy in your heart, loving our only Savior, check yourself. If you think Hillary should have won, so we wouldn't have had to trust Him to be Our Deliverer, check yourself. If you can't say, "Lord, not my will, but Your Will be done," check yourself.

"Though He slays me, yet will I trust Him." (Job 13:15(a), KJV).

I have no fear; I know Whose and who I am. Wake up and find out what He wants you to do to create a new Heaven and new Earth with Him. Try to truly give yourself away, so He can use you. But don't just sing about it, be about it. Don't boo, cry, blame, or be fearful. PRAY!

I recently read a post from a prophetess. In it she mentioned that God revealed to her that Trump was a man after His own heart. I have to admit, it was a little much for me to deal with and to accept. I've also had a hard time understanding that David was also called a man after His own heart. Or that Judas was not the disciple to whom Jesus said, "Get thee behind me Satan." Although, He did say several other negative things about Judas, including that he was the son of perdition (See John 17:12). In a Bible Study, at another local church, I was led to share how Judas played an important role in all our salvation. Dang, I think I've had so much empathy for Judas lately so I can learn to have it for Trump, too.

I was asking God to reveal to me what He is seeing in Trump. He was right, I wasn't ready to know. He showed me that I have a hard time seeing what He saw in some of my own family members, but I wanted to see it in Trump. He is merely revealing what is in the heart of the nation, men and, most of all, Christians. Now that the wound is open, maybe we can get the infection out. Jesus is our Healer!

I have to stop praying for my definition of perfect: nothing going on, no drama, no situations that would require God to do anything godly to fix. No requirements for me to be Christlike, if I don't feel like it. He is a big enough God to be God in any situation. We want to believe that everything we don't like is not of God, but what scripture can you find to back the opinion that God wants to keep us happy? No, He wants to transform us into His true image.

What did you choose for the 2016 election? I will speak about the 2020 election in *Bonus Week 6—46*. Did you choose the red pill (party) or the blue pill (party)? This is just from *Wikipedia.com* (don't judge me)! "The red pill and its opposite, the blue pill, are popular culture symbols representing the choice between embracing the, sometimes painful, truth of reality (red pill), and the blissful ignorance of illusion (blue pill). The terms, popularized in science fiction culture, are derived from the 1999 film, *The Matrix*."

I pray for Wisdom and to be like Him in these situations. Our Perfect God is better than anything bad!

Verses:

1 Samuel 8:18-20

1 Samuel 10:17-19

Genesis 6:5

Job 13:15

Proverbs 24:21-22

1 Timothy 2:1-3

Romans 13:1-5

Challenge:

Pray earnestly for our president, his family, and other elected government officials. Allow yourself to be obedient to the Word until your feelings catch up. Then, pray for and find a way to bless your enemy (yes, that one).

Prayer:

Father, please protect our Commander in Chief. Lord, I trust You completely. None of our U.S. elections have caught You by surprise because You planned them. Father show Your love, grace, and mercy to the Trump family. If he doesn't know You, let him have a real and true experience with You. Please take away any ill-feelings about any of Your people and any of Your plans that I don't like. Continue to perfect me in ways that challenge me and allow my flesh to die. I want to be more like You, and follow the example You showed us through the life of Jesus Christ, Our Lord and Savior. To the only wise God, Our Father be power and dominion forever. Amen!

My Notes

WEEK 46

The Most Powerful Prayer — Jesus!

I had several vivid dreams of being killed. I would yell out, "Jesus!" I remember one dream where I was shot in the face. The blood was covering my eyes. I knew I was dying and was unsure about my final resting place. I cried out for Jesus! It took several of these terrifying dreams to scare me, straight. I can be a little stubborn.

I began to realize that my unconscious and subconscious mind have been believing and crying out to Jesus for salvation. My cognizant mind needed to catch up to the revelation. It only took me a split second to recognize Jesus as my Savior in those dreams, but a bit longer for me to recognize this realization while I was awake.

We have to be careful not to assume we know God's redemption plan or that anyone is excluded from the plan. God is more powerful and knows more than any enemy. In my thoughts, I spent at least a decade disconnected from the church and from God. During that time, God was sure to keep watch over me like the Good Shepherd that He is.

It only takes a split second to be saved. We must not forget about the criminal hanging beside Jesus, who was told he would be in paradise with Jesus that very night. He didn't get baptized, he didn't do any rituals, he just recognized who he was with and was granted everlasting life. There is also a parable about the

Kingdom of Heaven. The landowner offered all the workers one-day's wage for their work. The workers who arrived later received the same payment as the ones who worked all day. The ones who worked longer expected more pay, but that is not what they received. It doesn't sound right or fair, but it is biblical and true.

I thank God that I don't get what I fairly deserve! I also thank Him that He gives everyone an opportunity to know Him and not be eternally separated from Him.

Verses:

Matthew 9:27-31

Matthew 20:10-16

Mark 1:16-20

Mark 5:41-42

Mark 7:25-30

Luke 18:35-43

Romans 9:15-16

Challenge:

Read the full parable of the workers in the vineyard from Matthew 20. Even consider reading the entire chapter for context. Allow God to show you more about His salvation plan. Be honest with yourself, and Him, about your feelings so He can open your eyes to see His Truth.

Prayer:

Lord, I am grateful that Your Word has the power to work immediately! Lord, I thank You for being my Savior when I wasn't even able to discern how far from You, I had strayed. I love You for opening my eyes and being good to me when I wasn't good to myself, others, or You. Amen!

My Notes

Cloud Atlas

I felt led to read the novel, titled *Cloud Atlas*, which is a book about the interrelated journey of reincarnated souls. Yesterday as I watched the sky, I took notice of how the clouds move and change shape. They permeate into each other, then separate, but they always keep moving. The book made a comparison between souls and the clouds.

As I am reading Exodus, I realize that The Good Book is making a similar comparison between the Glory of God and clouds. Clouds shade, bring rain, can obscure, and hide things in the natural. The Bible has many stories of the cloud being a signal to move or to stay in place. I'm waiting for more revelation on the clouds. All through the Bible, God reveals parts of His character through the main characters. He then comes in human flesh to show us how to be just like Him. Then, He dispenses His Holy Spirit to allow us to be just like Him. A similar thread flows through *Cloud Atlas*.

Verses:

Job 37:11-13

Exodus 13:21-22

Exodus 14:19-20

Exodus 24:15-18

Exodus 33:9-11

Exodus 40:34-38

Revelation 1:7-8

Challenge:

Be still and be amazed at what the Awesome Creator has created. Take time to watch the sunset over water, gaze up at the stars, or take in the beauty of a thunder or snowstorm. Find peace in whatever activity you choose and listen for the still, small Voice of God. Move when He tells you it's time to move.

Prayer:

Thank You for revealing Your majesty all around us, Lord. Help me to be mindful that You are ever-present with every cloud we see. You are awesome and amazing! I love You! Amen!

My Notes

Somewhere Under the Rainbow

I fell in a grocery store. Embarrassed, I rushed out, only to see the most vividly-colored double rainbow of my life. A few weeks later, my car was totaled. As I was purchasing a new car, I looked out and saw a rainbow peeking through the clouds. A few weeks after that, I was listening to Pandora and *Somewhere Over the Rainbow* came on. When I picked up the latest installment of my favorite book series, there was a rainbow on the front and a double full-circle rainbow on the back. Then, I turned on Pandora again a couple of days later and *I'll Trust You*, by Richard Smallwood, came on. There is a rainbow on that album cover as well. I guess God wants me to know more about rainbows!

This has been a tough year for many experiencing death, natural disasters, and many other tragedies. We are to be a light to someone who seems to have a dark stormy cloud in his or her life. I'm hopeful, I am bringing light to go with someone's rain, so that he or she can see a personal rainbow—God's promise for that person's life. I've had two separate occasions recently where people let me know that they left with big smiles on their faces, after we spent time together.

Sometimes I watch cartoons or read children's books as sort of a commercial break for life. According to the gospel of *The Care Bears*, "something good will come of the rain, just you wait!" I firmly believe that! Even Cheer Bear knows, "I just remembered what shows up after a rain shower, a rainbow!"

I was given this short prose poem:

The Rainbow's Treasure

We get to enjoy if we look up, look out, and look for it to catch the eye. If we are sucked into social media and local news, we miss it. If we look at what someone else was given, we may miss our treasure. The pot of gold is not at the end of the rainbow, but within the earthen vessels that God has given us, in which to temporarily dwell.

Verses:

Genesis 9:11-17

Leviticus 26:3-4

Deuteronomy 11:11-14

Deuteronomy 32:2

Ezekiel 1:28

Revelation 4:3

Revelation 10:1

Challenge:

Brighten someone's day! Take the time to be there for someone this week. There may or may not be something going on ,and you may or may not have any special words or gift to take to them. But you can share with them the promises of God—the rainbow that people need to see in the midst of a storm. Sometimes your presence is the only present needed.

Other ways we can meet each other's needs:

- » Go visit
- » Call
- » Text
- » Offer to babysit
- » Cook
- » Clean
- » Be limitless
- » Love
- » Peace
- » Grace
- » Mercy
- » Compassion

Prayer:

Lord, thank You for always adding sunshine to our rain and a silver lining to the clouds. Help us to realize the rain comes to provide us with what is needed for our growth, development, and maturation! I love You! Amen!

My Notes

WEEK 49

It's Already on the Calendar

A friend from church was instructed to set a time for prayer. In obedience, Kym Johnson Harden, author of *Trust God in the Light and in the Darkness*, sent out invitations for a few weeks out and put it on her calendar to take time to minister to her sisters. Shortly after the invitation went out, tragedy struck within our local church body. One of the sisters to whom, over the years, I have grown close—her husband was murdered. I was so grateful to have a time already set aside to gather in concert with other warriors who believe in the power of prayer. That Friday night, several of us gathered and lifted more than seventy people and their concerns into the mighty hand of Our Lord, Shepherd, Guide, and Healer. Several prayers were felt by those who needed the Holy Spirit to move and do what only He can accomplish, including the widow.

Most nights my sons, mom, and I are on a call praying and interceding. The list of prayer requests is never empty. It is good to know we have a standing appointment, to not only check in with each other, but also to talk to Our Father before bed.

I am so grateful for God putting things on the schedule for me: time to spend with me, time to wake me up, time to mature me, and time to love me. Sometimes I know about the appointment, date, interview, and sometimes I don't. But I am grateful that He has placed these things on my calendar. I know that He won't be late, and I know that He will never leave me nor forsake me, even until the end of the world.

Verses:

Exodus 13:10

Leviticus 23:2-4

Numbers 9:2-4

Psalm 75:2

Daniel 8:19

Matthew 16:3

Revelation 22:10

Challenge:

Set an alarm and put time on your calendar to spend time with God. Write something that He has revealed to you while in the secret place.

Prayer:

Thank You for being Almighty, but always mindful of me. Thank You for sending me a personal invitation and setting time to spend with me. I love You, Amen!

My Notes

WEEK 50

Delay in Delivery

I ordered several prayer journals about a month before Christmas 2018. Originally, I thought it would be here in time to be Christmas gifts. I didn't check the details in the confirmation email. I just expected, in this two-day delivery environment to which I have become so accustomed, that I would have them well before Christmas. A week or so later I realized I hadn't received them yet. So, I searched, actually I went back to read the email, and found out that the items were back-ordered and were scheduled to arrive right after Christmas. The next email I received announced that the journals would be delivered in late January, and the next delivery date was the middle of March. I was disappointed and a little frustrated.

I have successfully ordered and received many other things for myself and others, but that didn't have any bearings on this expected delivery. My next move was to remain hopeful that the devotionals would arrive at the perfect time for the recipients. I believe it was a timely delivery. I received them in time for a birthday celebration at a local first-of-its-kind breast health facility and intimates boutique, Cherry Blossom Intimates. I enjoyed giving the birthday girl, Kym, and everyone in the small group, this token of my affection. These are the prayer warriors mentioned in my Acknowledgments.

God has spoken a Word to me that has not come to fruition, yet. But I have to believe that it is still coming. Like the rain and the snow His Word will not return back void. It will accomplish what He sent it to do, at the appointed time. I do realize that God is training me in patience, and several other virtues, in the meantime. But I can't get the nagging feeling out of my head that the delay is somehow my fault. That feeling is confirmed by people who are well-intentioned, but not informed by God.

I feel like:

» I am on the back burner

» I have to come perfectly, or very close to it, without being a know-it-all to receive

» There is some secret formula and always a reason why it's not time

» I did something wrong, said something wrong, felt something wrong, and that something is delaying the arrival or answer to my prayer

I have acknowledged how I feel. But I have to act on what I know. I am not wrong or being punished for not hitting submit just right. I am being fully prepared to be a good thing more precious than rubies at the perfect time. Blessings, like deliveries, aren't just for the perfect! The ones who are still being perfected are still deemed worthy to receive good things from God.

Verses:

James 1:17-18

Matthew 7:11

John 3:27

Psalm 84:11

Isaiah 54: 7-8

Isaiah 63:7

Nehemiah 9:30-31

Challenge:

Write down the promise that you have been believing God for. Be mindful of ways that you are maturing as you await the delivery of the promise. Are you more patient, kind, loving, etc. in situations where you previously did not display spiritual fruit?

Prayer:

Lord, Your ways and timing are perfect. Please help me to remember that delay is not denial. You have spoken it, and You are faithful. Every good gift comes from You. I appreciate that you are preparing me for the delivery and have already prepared the delivery for me. Amen!

My Notes

The Warrior's Arsenal

When storms and rainy weather come, I don't always know what to say.

A friend of mine, Mary Smith, lost her granddaughter and two sons, all within one month in 2018. The granddaughter was stillborn. Her sons were lost due to gun violence. After hearing about the second son's murder, who was the father of her stillborn granddaughter, I was completely speechless! I felt like I had nothing to offer this friend in such a time of grieving, but earnest prayers from afar for peace, love, and comfort. I felt it wasn't enough. However, I was reminded prayer is powerful not passive.

I wanted to be sunshine in her rain, but I really felt like I had nothing to give and nothing to say during this time. I was not fortified in the scriptures. I didn't have the words that can bring new life.

Another friend of hers had the right words coming from Jesus, our God, our Savior, our Comforter, and our Healer. I pray that the words heal her and her family in a way that only God can. I'm hopeful those who are called by His Name, will stand in the gap for the heartbroken. Next time, I want to stand ready to be His hands, His feet, and His mouthpiece—equipped to give a loving hug, food, finances, the words of life, or whatever support is needed.

A lot of people only say R.I.P. when someone dies. I think rest-in-peace is for the living. God is close to the brokenhearted. He will give peace and sweet rest in the midst of any storm. Our words are powerful. God's Word is all-powerful. Both she and I were reminded of the promises of God through the following verses in her friend's Facebook post.

Verses:

Psalm 34:19

Psalm 31:9

Psalm 147:3

Matthew 5:4

John 14:27

John 14:18

Psalm 46:1

Challenge:

Prepare your arsenal with at least seven scriptures, so the light can shine through you in the midst of a storm. Memorize them, hide them in your heart, so you will have them ready when needed. We speak life and truth!

Prayer:

Holy Spirit, please intercede and translate tears, moans, and groans into a prayer to the Father. According to John 17:17, please sanctify us in the truth. Your Word is the Truth. Jesus, thank You! Father God, You are still good! Amen!

My Notes

The Perfect Storm

"When you were born, the worst thunderstorm I've ever seen came through!"

I've heard this story from my mom at least once a year, on every birthday since I can remember. I have been given the ability to change climates and atmospheres. Much like a storm I can be tempestuous, cleansing, shaking, stirring, destructive, or calming. It just depends on the mood I am in. At my worst, I can shake things up and ensure there is chaos.

But I have also been able to usher in the presence of the True and Living God, to bring peace where there was none. I have an affinity to Storm in the *X-Men*, I like the way she uses storm elements to fight the good fight, and she reps for the melanin-rich power-house sisters. However, God has shown to me, during our quiet time, that I am more like Jean Gray. This character feels everything from everybody— I can definitely relate. I don't know how to move things with my mind, but I know that I can speak to a mountain and it will move, it's good enough for me.

I AM, told me that I am:

- » Warrior Bride
- » Gatekeeper
- » Prophetic Intercessor
- » Pollinator
- » Chosen

- » Healer
- » A prayer, come true
- » Spiritual Thermostat
- » Worthy of doing God's work
- » Genius
- » Gifted
- » Lily—not just of the valley
- » Salt
- » Light
- » Powerful
- » Moderator
- » Educator
- » Innovator

And He also shared this short poem with me:

Untitled

Daughter, I am here I never leave.

Why is that hard for you to believe?

My presence doesn't mean you won't go through,

Even in the valley of the shadow of death, I am with you.

I planted you in valleys for seasons to beautify, purify, and reveal truth!

Verses:

Revelation 19:11-16

Isaiah 43:1

Exodus 33:17

Isaiah 62:2

Isaiah 9:6

Song of Solomon 2:1-2

1 Kings 7:22

Challenge:

Write down, "I AM" and let I Am, write a love letter to you and tell you who He created you to be. Go back and look at your challenge responses and any questions or prayers that you recorded throughout the book. Were there topics that you struggled to grasp either the meaning or concept? Did you live out the challenges? Were the noted prayer requests answered? Is there anything else that should be added to your testimony? Now that I have given my gift it is now completely up to you, are you going to share your testimony with someone and let it be a life-giving gift of love or are you going to keep it to yourself?

God loves you and so do I!

Prayer:

God, please help me to use my gifts, talents, strength, and power to bring You greater glory and for the good of the Kingdom. Amen!

My Notes

Part Three

BONUS WEEK 1

Listen to Him and him

So, I'm a talker. We have many, many generations of talkers in my family. Get me on the phone and it will be at least an hour before you can get me off! This is how I am with my inner- circle. However, if I'm uncomfortable you will just get one sentence out of me and that is probably it.

As God is preparing me for my husband, He told me, "This is My son, with him I am well pleased," then He asked me what was next. I couldn't remember, so I looked it up. Two verses talk about Jesus being led by the Holy Spirit to be tested. Two verses instruct me to listen to Him. I prayed that my husband is strong and mighty, remembering who God is and who he is in God throughout any test. I also took heed to my instruction to learn to listen better. I need to listen fully, undistracted, without planning what I am going to say next, without having to have a word of wisdom, or a solution for this situation. I just need to be able to listen to the heart of the man God has designed me to be with, without me trying to save or fix!

I must admit, sometimes I have a hard time listening to God and incorporating all He tells me as The Truth. I know God is infallible and my husband will not be. I have to listen to God and my husband. I must allow them to lead and guide me. I must let them fly this plane and I must have a seat! In turbulence, I will buckle my seatbelt and pray, and not go knocking on the cockpit door making sure everything is okay. We will arrive safely at our destiny! When he gets home, he will hear, "Well done, good and faithful servant!" And so, will I!

I love my husband, already. I will listen to Him and him!

Verses:

Mark 9:7

Matthew 17:5

Mark 1:11

Matthew 3:17

2 Peter 1:16-21

Deuteronomy 18:15

Genesis 21:12

Challenge:

Sit quietly, ask God to speak because His servant is listening. Write what He shares with you.

Prayer:

Lord, please help me to be quick to listen, slow to speak, and slow to anger, according to Your Word in James 1:19. Holy Spirit, arrest my tongue when it is tempted to speak words that don't bring light or life to a situation. In Jesus' Name! Amen!

My Notes

The Sewing Lesson With My Mom and Our Father

I received some African-inspired printed material from one of my closest friends, Helen Bryant. And I decided I was going to make a skirt instead of spending about sixty dollars for the ones that I have seen in stores. *How hard could it be?* It's basically the front, back, and two seams. I went to a fabric store, searched through the pattern books, found something that I thought I would like and be able to make, and picked up a dress pattern. Yeah, I changed my skirt to a dress, and I was thinking, *I'm ready*.

Then, I read the packaging and realized I needed additional sewing notions. I went back to the store to get the zipper and clasp hook sets. *Now I'm ready*. I set an appointment with my mom—my personal, semi-pro seamstress—and I was definitely ready to make this dress! My mom checked the machine to make sure it still ran properly. Then my appointment time came.

I was all excited, until I had to read the instructions. The sheets looked like engineering or architecture blueprints to me. I just wanted to make a dress! My mom walked me through getting the proper pieces for my dress pattern … Now, *I was ready* … Then she told me to cut out the pattern pieces and pin them to the material. Okay, *now am I ready to make my dress?!* Nope, then I had to cut the material, remove the pattern, re-read the instructions, re-pin so I could sew, make darts and pleats. I was completely frustrated and on the edge of tears about this dress. This was not just a sewing lesson.

While I was frustrated, God gently whispered something to me about being this frustrated with trying to get the fabric sewn together. Meanwhile, I was telling Him I am ready for marriage. I was clearly neither ready to make this dress nor ready to make a marriage *work*. But thankfully, He is always ready and doing so many things to prepare me for all His future plans.

Instead of being so caught up in the how and when, I can just rest assured that the Who has spoken to me can never lie or fail! Eventually, the dress will be complete, but as of right now, it is hanging in my closet waiting for me to get my nerve together to finish what I asked for and began. Good thing my salvation doesn't depend on me. The One who came to author and finish my faith is so much better at following instructions and finishing than I am.

Verses:

Hebrews 12:2

Genesis 3:7

Job 16:15

Mark 10:9

Psalm 119:173

Revelation 19:7

Revelation 21:2

Challenge:

Is there a process that God can talk you through as you are trying to complete it? Really listen for a whisper as you do something that may not be the easiest for you to accomplish. Let Him help you to see a deeper meaning in all you put your hands to do this week.

Prayer:

Lord, please steady my hands and let me hear Your voice directing, leading, and guiding me! Amen!

My Notes

The Snapping Turtle
and Her Seed

When my son was about eight or nine, he got a new bike, but he had yet to master the gears that would allow him to conquer the hills in our neighborhood. This caused us to detour from our normal walking path just following the sidewalks. Instead we followed the path as far as he could manage, then we doubled back over the same sidewalks on the way home.

I had an unexpected experience while on one walk. I was getting tired and felt like skipping the last cul-de-sac and going home more directly. However, my son was in front of me, so I followed him as he turned off the main road to continue the sidewalk path. A gentleman was outside, and I decided to speak. I don't always speak. He was watching a turtle laying her eggs in a nest she built. I've never seen anything like it, and I wanted my son to see this also. After I caught up with my son, we both watched the rest of the process. The turtle laid her eggs in a space she had cleared in the man's yard, covered them, and went back to the nearby stream.

The gentleman chose beautiful words to describe her actions, "She lays the eggs and then lets the sun (Son) do its work!"

I loved hearing those words while we were, and still are, working on the patio garden and other life projects. My son thought it was weird behavior for the mom to just leave her young and go on about her business, never going back to check on them. The gentleman actually juxtaposed the situation for us with the practices of an alligator, who does return to check on her young and is, as he described, "more motherly," than the snapping turtle.

Now that I've had a little more time to think on it, the snapping turtle was being very motherly and very much like Our Loving Father! He will leave us to His Son, the Author and Finisher of our faith and not immediately rescue us out of situations that are dark, dirty, and undesirable to us. He has shown me that I am a person who doesn't like to stand by as people go through. It may not sound like a bad quality, initially, but I would like to shield people from things that have been put in place for growth, development, and maturation.

I was shown a scripture about burdens and loads. If God has given someone a load that is too heavy, they are instructed to take it to the Everlasting Arm. Be a friend, direct your friend, loved one or even yourself to Jesus to unload. However, with burdens we are directed to help each other out. Helpers only help, not fix. We cannot change others' circumstances or loads. I need to understand that if God is not allowing the protection, grace, increase, or whatever I think is needed, then there is nothing that I can do in the situation. I need to step back and let God do what He does best, while always listening for Him to direct me.

Are you blocking the Son or allowing Him to do His perfect work? Are we standing strong in the fact that God is all wise or do we think He needs us to be Holy Ghost, Jr.?

Verses:

Deuteronomy 1:12

Nehemiah 4:16-17

Galatians 6:2 & 5

Ephesians 4 :1-2

Matthew 11:28-30

Numbers 11:17

Psalm 55:22

Challenge:

Pray that God will open your eyes to ways that you are attempting to block His moves or when you do not fully trust that He has it all covered.

Prayer:

Lord, remind us to come to You when our burdens and loads are too much to bear on our own. I know sometimes, You will raise up Your remnant or use people who don't even acknowledge You to help me. Sometimes You move in a way that I have to stop and recognize Your hand, awesome strength, and majesty. Amen!

My Notes

BONUS WEEK 4

Baby Watch — Are You Expecting?

In June 2016, I spent some time with one of my closest girlfriends, Alisa Sheard, as she was expecting a new baby. Everyone assumed she would have the baby well before the due date, since her belly had grown so large. When we still had a couple of days before the due date, everyone, especially my friend, was more than ready for the big debut. Everything had been purchased or retrieved from storage, clothes had been washed and put away, and the room was painted. The only thing was that the baby was clearly not ready—yet. It didn't mean her bundle never came; it just meant that the fullness of time had not come yet. When I spoke with her briefly, she was understandably a little frustrated. However, she had chosen to take this time to relax and rest.

What about you? I'll be honest and say I have yet to master this skill. I am learning to rest while I wait for the fullness of time to get here. Once I am sure that I have completed the prescription perfectly prescribed by the Master Physician, I need to sit back and relax knowing that God is doing what is necessary for what He has spoken to come to full fruition. I am trying to patiently wait and not to be anxious for anything. And I certainly didn't want to cause my friend to be anxious while she was waiting on her new arrival, who arrived perfectly at the appointed time.

Verses:

Philippians 4:6-8

Psalm 37:7

Psalm 40:1

Hebrews 6:13-18

Genesis 49:18

Numbers 9:18

Ruth 3:18

Challenge:

Write out the prescription that God has asked you to follow, even if it seems to have no correlation to the promise, He has spoken to you. Follow your prescription!

Prayer:

Lord, help me to diligently follow what You have told me to do while I wait and wait and wait for the fullness of time for a specific promise. I want to be perfectly prepared for this blessing. I know I heard You, clearly, and You do not lie, I believe You according to Your Word in Hebrews 6:17-18. In Jesus' Name! Amen

My Notes

BONUS WEEK 5

A Whole Lot to Learn at Lotte Mart — International Market

My sons and I fell in love with an international market named, Lotte Mart. Occasionally, we take the forty-plus minute ride each way and share a special lunch of cheap, fresh, delicious sushi. There is so much fresh produce, meat, and seafood at the market that it sometimes put me in overload. We have a common practice of talking about what we learned or what stood out to us after we've experienced different things. And we did the same after this one trip to the market.

I shared that I thought it was awesome that you could buy every part of the plant: the root, the seeds or nuts, and the flesh or fruit. We also saw produce at different levels or maturity: young green, ripe, and dried. It is a different state of mind than I am used to, which causes others to think of how to use every part of a plant. We usually go straight for the flesh and throw the rest away. If I had my way, my produce would be at the peak of ripeness and perfectly unblemished. At times, I have taken so long to pick apples that God had the time to talk and correct me.

"If you take the most beautiful ones for yourself, what are you leaving for everyone else?"

I also saw varieties of fruits and vegetables that I am not used to. We also commented on how this was the first time we had seen some of these foods in person.

Maybe that's why we can't fathom our God using anything that isn't exactly like us, or who we pretend to be. God has the ability to use us all. Since God doesn't seem to discard what we deem undesirable, maybe we shouldn't be so quick to either.

Verses:

Ecclesiastes 3:11

Psalm 128:1-4

Genesis 1:31

Song of Solomon 2:3

Ezekiel 36:30

Jeremiah 12:2

Philemon 1:10-14

Challenge:

Allow God to show you at least one treasure that He has placed in someone or yourself that you have written off or undervalued. Repent for devaluing the Master's creation.

Prayer:

Lord, please help me to see the value of everyone in my realm of influence. Please don't let me be so quick to dismiss them for not living up to my standards! Allow me to appreciate the beauty, even if it is hiding. In Jesus' Name! Amen!

My Notes

BONUS WEEK 6

46

The 2020 election had done more than reveal division in the country. It revealed the division in the church. It exposed what had been swept under a rug and not dealt with. Some card-carrying Christians haven't spoken to God in a very long time. Not only are we not speaking to God, but we aren't listening either.

"For a Child will be born to us, a Son will be given to us; And the government will rest on His shoulders; And His name will be called Wonderful Counselor, Mighty God, Eternal Father, Prince of Peace." (Isaiah 9:6, NASB)

What has changed in the church since the election of 2016? What did you choose for the 2020 election? Did you choose the red pill (party) or the blue pill (party)? Are we abiding in His government, or in the Republicans vs Democrats government? How did you feel after you found out that Biden had been declared president?

Christians claim to have one God. But Christians can be heard reporting that either Trump is the anti-Christ and Biden is our savior, or conversely likening Trump to Jesus and saying Biden will usher in the beast. These despairing messages are reportedly directly from God. *The Democrats are delusional, don't know God, and committed voter fraud. The Republicans are delusional, don't know God, and committed voter suppression.*

"And for this reason God will send upon them a deluding influence so that they might believe what is false." (2 Thessalonians 2:11, NASB)

I've heard all of the above. Honestly, I don't know which is true. How would I know, especially since I didn't ask God? I don't have a political bone in my body. As best as I can tell, neither party cares much about Suzanne, nor her Black sons, so I am not looking to them to do much in my life. Neither has fruit that appears like the Holy Spirit from my vantage point. But my perspective may be off. If I put them under a magnifying glass, microscope or telescope, the random pieces that I focus on may not look very godly. But don't worry, I did exercise my right to vote, my son and I both voted early. I even googled to find out who had won the 2020 election more times than I care to remember.

How would people judge us if our filter was broken and our inner thoughts became the nightly news headlines. What about if the hot mic spilled the beans and told the message your unsaved face tries to hold in. What would everyone think if your mask fell off and everyone was privy to how you really act when you are at home, and you think nobody is watching. Just like these candidates are being watched; we are, too.

I once had a dream. I was just an observer of a large group of people in the water and another large group on the shore, looking at the group in the water. The people in the water started fighting. Shortly afterwards, people on the shore also started to fight. I believe this represented the Body in the water and the world on the shore. If we are fighting amongst ourselves and we claim to be His, what chance does the world have?

Those who call themselves by His Name are divided, leaving nasty messages for each other in the comments section of prophetic videos, sentencing each other to Hell. Leaving everyone behind to deal with God's wrath, as they get whisked off to a pre-or-mid-tribulation rapture. We are divided between lovers of self, and lovers of God. This foolishness must stop! We have to start practicing what we preach while we still have time. The whole world is watching the U.S. and us. Even those who only claim His Name are being watched. If we love God, He says we would keep His commandments. What is the greatest commandment according to Jesus?

"And He said to him, 'You shall love the Lord your God with all your heart, and with all your soul, and with all your mind.' This is the great and foremost commandment. The second is like it, 'You shall love your neighbor as yourself.'" (Matthew 22:37-39, NASB)

The church is divided. So, of course, the USA is divided. As of this writing, the popular vote is history in the making, with a little more than 73 million votes to the republican candidate and a little more than 80 million to the democratic candidate. No matter who is the president, the beliefs and opinions of this many staunchly opposing U.S. citizens won't just go away when a leader is sworn in.

But God does care! I am looking to the author and finisher of my faith. Jesus is my Lord, the Father is the Lover of my soul, the Holy Spirit is my Comforter and Guide. God uses whom He wishes, how He wishes. God is sovereign and He has the final say in the raising and lowering of kings. I have no fear; I know Whose and who I am.

Wake up and find out what He wants you to do to create a new Heaven and new Earth with Him. Try to truly give yourself away, so He can use you. But don't just sing about it, be about it. Don't boo, cry, blame, or be fearful. PRAY! But we have to stop praying for our definition of perfect: nothing going on, no drama, no situations that would require God to do anything godly to fix. No requirements for us to be Christlike if we don't feel like it. He is a big enough God to be God in any situation. We want to believe that everything we don't like is not of God, but what scripture can you find to back the opinion that God wants to keep us happy? No, He wants to transform us into His true image.

If this message seems familiar, it is. Instead of updating *Week 45—A Man After God's Own Heart—a Jagged Pill*. I was instructed to reuse part of that devotional to create this devotional for the most recent election. I pray for Wisdom and to be like Him in these situations. Our Perfect God is better than anything bad!

Verses:

1 Samuel 8:18-20

1 Samuel 10:17-19

Genesis 6:5

Job 13:15

Proverbs 24:21-22

1 Timothy 2:1-3

Romans 13:1-5

Challenge:

Pray earnestly for our president, his family, and other elected government officials. Allow yourself to be obedient to the Word until your feelings catch up. Then, pray for and find a way to bless your enemy (yes, that one).

Prayer:

Father, please protect our Commander in Chief. Lord, I trust You completely. None of our U.S. elections have caught You by surprise because You planned them. Father show Your love, grace, and mercy to the Biden family. If he doesn't know You, let him have a real and true experience with You. Please take away any ill-feelings about any of Your people and any of Your plans that I don't like. Continue to perfect me in ways that challenge me and allow my flesh to die. I want to be more like You and follow the example You showed us through the life of Jesus Christ, Our Lord and Savior. To the only wise God, Our Father be power and dominion forever. Amen!

My Notes

The New Earth

On a regular basis, I tend to have these communal-type dreams where everyone works together and lives in large compounds like one big family. Some of the people I know, currently, but a lot of them I don't, yet no one feels like a stranger. There is community with unity, peace, love, and joy everywhere. There are no hard boundaries. There is no mine and no yours. There is neither money nor the love of it. Many things are missing, but instead of listing them all, I'd rather focus on how beautiful it feels. We truly love each other and do what is best for the group. Gifts and talents are used in harmony to advance us all. These dreams show me Acts 2:44 and 4:32-35 in living color.

On the other side, all this painful groaning and messy childbirth is worth it. I know we will see the New Earth. Holy Spirit, please be our midwife!

I was given this to think about:

In my Father's house there are many mansions.

On Earth as it is in Heaven.

What are you doing with yours?

Is your door opened or closed to those in need?

Can they come in and taste and see that the Lord is good through interaction with you?

Is it a house of prayer or an annex to the synagogue of Satan?

Is it Heaven or Hell?

A catalyst for peace or war?

Does light shine out or is it a black hole?

When someone stops by, do they know you're a Christian by your love, kindness, graciousness or acts of service?

Verses:

John 14:2-3

1 Kings 8:27-29

Isaiah 56:7-8

Luke 19:46

Revelation 2:9

Revelation 3:7-9

2 Peter 3:10-18

Challenge:

Ask God how you can come to Him with unity within the family, church, or community in which you are currently positioned to be a change agent. Let Him show you how to bring Heaven to Earth. As a bonus read Acts 2 and Acts 4.

Prayer:

Holy Spirit, please be our midwife. Make the Earth look like Heaven through Your Body, Remnant, Bride, and Presence! In Jesus' Name! Amen!

My Notes

BONUS WEEK 8

Home Again

I was very fortunate to be blessed with a home at the end of 2017. The Lord ensured that the thing, I thought was standing in the way of me being a homeowner, would be the thing to qualify me for a special homeownership program. Student loan debt was a requirement for a new mortgage program in my state. I not only became a homeowner, but also my student loan balance was paid off in the process! Let me take a moment to Thank God, because I know this blessing is from Him! Hallelujah! Thank You, Father!!

I spent the night in my new house the day I settled, and every night until this incident. The house was about twenty years old and had some things that needed a little work. My air conditioner was one of the areas that needed a little more love. Moving in during the winter, followed by a mild spring meant that my air conditioner (my AC) didn't really have to run much until May.

One day I went downstairs and noticed my carpet was wet. I found more water when I opened the closet that housed my air conditioner unit, water heater, and my washer and dryer. I contacted my home warranty company, immediately. The HVAC tech came and reported that the condensation ring had been clogged. He fixed it, I paid my deductible, and he left. No more leaking!

I was satisfied for a few weeks. As the weather started getting hotter, I noticed certain areas of my house were not very cool. One evening while cooking dinner, my company commented, "Is the AC on?!"

"Yeah, it's on!" I responded, assuming that cooking was making the house so warm.

We hit a few days of hot and humid weather and I noticed my air conditioner was running constantly, but the temperature was no longer comfortable in the bedrooms on the top level. I called the HVAC company again but was told it was a separate issue, and I had to pay a new deductible. The same technician came but this time, I made sure he was more thorough. He checked the inside unit, the temperature from the vents, the system layout, and he cleaned the outside unit. I turned on the unit, there was cool air coming out but not cold air. Slowly the temperature started to creep down.

Hours later, the unit was still running, and the temperature had only dropped a few degrees. I called back and was told to just let the system run.

"Is it healthy for the system to run like that?" I asked.

"It's fine. Just let it run overnight and things will cool off!"

"Okay!" I replied, skeptically.

I ran it for hours, but then decided to cut it off and was hopeful the temperature would lower by the morning. Overnight, I thought I heard something falling and crashing, but I was half sleep and not sure about it. The next day the AC ran for hours, only to lower the temperature by about three degrees. Then the system would cut off for about fifteen minutes, and then stay on again for an hour or so.

Not happy, I called the company again. They set up an appointment for later that day. The techs arrived in the evening, after running the AC, most of the day, to maintain a temp around eighty degrees. They came and rechecked the inside and outside units. The tech quickly returned to tell me there was a problem, ice. The unit had frozen. The ice defrosting from the unit caused the crashing sound I heard. But they wouldn't be able to return until tomorrow at the earliest to fix it. I was done with this hot house and had to go!

I am fortunate to live about twenty minutes away from my very generous parents. They received me with open arms! I noticed the force of their AC unit right away. Leading me to understand what was going on at my house, the unit lacked power. At my house, you had to stand directly under the vents to feel anything cool. Armed with this new perspective, I went back to the HVAC company.

Having an air conditioner is much different than using it. On a hot day, merely possessing an air conditioner doesn't provide relief. What's the point of having an air conditioning unit but it's not working properly? So, eventually, I got a new AC unit.

The religious system I was living with lacked the power to be effective. I had gotten used to the weak system until things froze up on me and just stopped working. With God we can gain a new perspective, we don't have to stay the prodigal. Don't be too proud to get the help you need. Our Father is All-Powerful, ready and more than equipped to help us through all of life's situations.

Verses:

Joel 2:12-13

Jeremiah 3:12-14 & 22

Philippians 3:18-21

Ephesians 2:19-22

2 Corinthians 5:1-2

Mark 6:12

1 Peter 2:25

Challenge:

Ask God to help you with the answers to the following questions:

How is the religious system serving you? Does it arm you with the ability to shift environments, heal, love, and learn? Or is it lukewarm, allowing just enough relief to barely get you to the next service, event, or conference?

Prayer:

God, please illuminate the path to help me come home to You again. Also, while I am on my journey, help me to show others the way into the Kingdom. I love You. Amen!

My Notes

BONUS WEEK 9

No Guarantees

My family is loyal. If my dad isn't still using the original product, he hasn't strayed too far from it. In all the time that I've known him, I've only seen him use up to three brands of any given product. When he does make a change, it's because there has been a big change in formula, or the product is no longer around, or sometimes the whole company is gone. For example, I watched him change from Tone soap to Dove. Jergens lotion to Vaseline Intensive Care. Sunlight dish detergent, to Ajax, to Dawn. He recently retired Magic Shave and Sta-Sof-Fro, I think it was because he had such a difficult time finding them.

In the late '90s my first cell phone was with Cingular Wireless. Do you remember that company? I barely remember. With an acquisition, we got grandfathered into AT&T, many moons ago, and stayed with them for well over a decade. Around Christmas 2018, we moved the family plan to a new cell phone provider. We wanted new phones and T-Mobile had a plan, honoring veterans—like my dad. We all got the latest phones and some other perks for less than our current bill with AT&T. I gave them one last chance to keep our business, but they couldn't compete with this deal.

During the switch, we ensured we did everything to make sure we would receive the proper credits and promotions. We turned in the correct forms, mailed the phones, and did whatever else was required. However, months later my line was still not receiving the proper monthly credit for the promotion. I called at least seven times, during the process, and was assured by each representative that, although I had received a text or email to the contrary, I would still receive the program's full benefits and proper monthly account credit. Many times, I expressed the desire to have proof that I was to receive what I was promised by the representatives. But each time I received more information from the representative, they continued to claim that they could provide no actual proof.

A couple of months later, my bill was still not being credited properly, and I called again. This time, I was told that I didn't meet the promotion requirements by the deadline and there was nothing that could be done to ensure I received the proper credit for my phone. It took several additional months, and many more calls, before the situation was remedied.

In conversation, I shared that I wanted a guarantee. If I fell in love, would there be a guarantee that the other person would fulfill an unspoken, unwritten list, formulated, and fantasized about in my mind? However, life has no guarantees like that. I want the person to be loyal just like my family is loyal. But people can promise, lie, have best intentions, fail, not know what they are doing, not be recognized or appreciated for what they do, and the list goes on. To me that is scary! So, I would like a written guarantee, and I want that person to have no ability to go back on his word. But that would not allow me to Trust God, lean not on my understanding, acknowledge Him, and get my path directed by God who comes with a guarantee.

He says, "… I will never leave you, nor forsake you …"

He says, "… nothing can separate you from His love …"

He says, "… love never fails …"

The guarantees that I do have are so much better than what anyone can even hope to promise or dare to fulfill.

Verses:

Deuteronomy 31:6-8

Joshua 1:5

1 Kings 8:57

1 Chronicles 28:20

Isaiah 42:16

Romans 8: 35-39

1 Corinthians 13:8

Challenge:

Think of an old product, toy, or food item that you used to enjoy, but it is no longer available. Think about what replaced that item in your life. Think about an old childish way, sin, or habit that you used to, or may still, enjoy. Allow God to show you how to replace that idol with something life-giving.

Prayer:

Dear God, please help me to love my fellow man by trusting You. I trust You to make every crooked place straight. I trust You to illuminate my path. I trust You even when the path goes through the valley where the shadow of death is. I trust You to rebuild my heart even if it is mishandled. I trust You and I love You. Amen!

My Notes

BONUS WEEK 10

Shut Down or Restart

This morning both of my work computers were experiencing issues. One never got to the login screen. The other seemed like it was fine, but I realized I wasn't able to connect with my Outlook program to get emails. I decided to start over. I turned off one computer. Then I tried shutting down the other. I realized that out of my options: sleep, shut down, or restart, I usually choose the *shut down* option even when I know I will actually be restarting the computer.

The same is true with my life. When challenging times come, storms hit, or the enemy attacks, I feel I have to shut down or want to go to sleep. I don't want to pray, read, write, worship, encourage, intercede, or fellowship. I just want to wallow. I try desperately, and usually fail, trying to figure out what is wrong. I did *x, y, and z*, just like I was told, and still this undesired thing happened. This does not compute! This is not what I was taught. Go to church, pray, give, serve and God will protect you, your family and your stuff.

This morning, I woke up with the word *despondent* in my head. I had to look it up and unfortunately, it matched what I had been feeling for the past several days: feeling or showing extreme discouragement, dejection, or depression. This should not be, I couldn't stay there. *Almighty God*, was playing in my spirit as I woke up. So, I went to YouTube and pulled up the play list. The songs ministered to me, reminding me that God is still almighty. No situation is beyond His repair. His healing touch can, and will, heal every hurt, pain, disappointment, grief, and fear.

Why did this thing happen to me, my family, my friends, and my loved ones? It doesn't make sense. In my spirit, God spoke to me about this: *If bad things only happen in families where no one is praying and believing, how would healing happen?* I still think it is unfair, but it actually makes perfect sense. How would a nonbeliever learn to be victorious if we are unwilling to be an example? Jesus chose not to take the easy way out. I feel like I was taught that He sacrificed so I can take easy street. But the Bible teaches us to take up our cross, daily. To die to ourselves. To be a living sacrifice. That seems to match what most disciples experience in their walk.

I can't shut down. I have to finish the race that I have started. Although I don't like what I see, I have to reboot, and restart so that I can get to my destiny. The prize will not be won if I just shut down, lie down, and give up. These devotionals remind me that the victory is won as we continue to press forward. The journey may take us through the valley where the shadow of death is, but we must continue to go through wherever Our Shepherd leads us.

I even shared with my mom that I can see why people lose faith, based on the teaching that I previously chose to believe. But I can't renounce my faith. He has brought me through too much. He will bring us through this valley, too. There is healing for the soul! I claim it, now, by faith and not by sight. I have to keep doing the things that I know are right, whether I receive my intended result or not. It is all working together, not just for my good, but for the good of all of those who love Him and are called according to His purpose, and not our own.

Verses:

1 Kings 21:27

Philippians 3:12-16

Romans 11:29

2 Corinthians 4:16-18

Ephesians 4:23

Psalm 51:10

Romans 8:6

Challenge:

Remember a time or situation in your life that you thought you would never make it through, only to acknowledge that God saw you through yet another victory. Write the story from the victor's perspective—that's you!

Prayer:

God, thank You, for challenging times that remind us that you are all-powerful, and that we are more than conquerors through You. In Jesus' Name! Amen!

My Notes

Money Is a Tool, Like a Hammer

Think about how many hammers you own. Imagine if it became a social norm to stockpile hammers, accumulating as many as you could get your hands on. After getting all your hammers, imagine your neighbor needed to borrow one. Would you gladly let him or her borrow or even have a hammer, or would you think your neighbor needs to get his or her own?

God has allowed me to see that money is simply a tool. It is very useful and needed in our society since we moved beyond the barter system and on to currency. However, just because it has importance, it doesn't change the use for which it was created.

What are you doing with the tools you have been given? We have gifts, talents, and tools to help others in the Body, and also to show other people who God is, through our interactions with them. We don't have to hoard in order to make it. That is outside of God's Will. He teaches us to give and it will be given to us.

"If you give to others, you will be given a full amount in return. It will be packed down, shaken together, and spilling over into your lap. The way you treat others is the way you will be treated." (Luke 6:38, CEV)

Since we consider ourselves His Body, we must operate as such. What part of your body hoards all the cells, blood, or nutrients? Why do we feel our fists must be closed so tightly around what we think we own, in order to have what we need? God allows for our needs to be met. Our job is not to worry about that, and to be willing to listen to how He is instructing us to use the tools He has provided.

Verses:

Ecclesiastes 5:10

Psalm 37:16

Hebrews 13:5

Matthew 19:21

Luke 12:33

Deuteronomy 15:7-8

1 Samuel 2:7-8

Challenge:

Give! Not pocket change. Not a little ... but a lot. Either give a little more than you feel like you would normally want to, more than you think you are able, or much more than you feel the person deserves. Give what you would want to be given in a similar situation.

Prayer:

God, please help me to be as generous as You are with me. You loved so much that You gave Your Only Son for us. I desire to be perfected in this area of my life. I want to live, knowing that I have been blessed to be a blessing to someone else. Help me to fight the urge to be stingy. Let me give with an abundance just as You have shown me. I love You and thank You for loving me so much! Amen!

My Notes

Stretch Marks — Visibly Marked by Growth, or Flawless

My sister gave me a photo shoot so that I can have professional headshots from which I could choose my author's photo for the back cover of *The Gift, Unveiled*. The end-result was a striking series of pictures that most people described as stunning, beautiful, fabulous, and flawless. However, I didn't wake up like this! It took hours of getting my hair done by Ms. Didi Green of Network Hair. Over an hour getting a "natural glam" by celebrity makeup artist Kenya Rucker @basedkenken. It took hours of smiling, posing, turning, while Jasmine was setting the stage, walking, squatting, climbing, and lifting to capture the perfect angles.

My make-up was so flawless I was shocked as I stared at a slightly familiar face in the mirror. My neighbor of three years, Tarsha, barely recognized me. I was concerned that my phone wouldn't recognize my face, and I would have to put in my passcode to unlock my phone, but fortunately it did.

One of my photos was so flawless that my Aunt Billie thought the person smiling back at her was someone else. "She looks a little like Suzie," my aunt said to my cousin, Brandi, her daughter. Puzzled, my aunt asked, "Is that why you sent this to me?"

I'm hopeful you recognize me in the streets with my twist-out self-styled hair, in my comfy jeans and a T-shirt.

Suzanne L. Williams | 287

What did I see in the make-up artist's video? I zeroed in on my not flat stomach. In the sneak-peek photo in my phone, I saw my gap and keloids. But I decided I was not going to give my sister the huge task of trying to clone perfect skin in Photoshop, especially since she had already gifted me a free photo shoot. So, I was going to leave my scars visible because I am slightly scarred.

I woke up in the middle of the night to a text, from my friend, Joy. She sent a text from a post sharing the beauty of kintsugi pottery. This style fills in the cracks and imperfections with gold. It doesn't seek to hide the flaws. It accentuates the flaws. The gold is not only beautiful, but it fortifies the pottery making it stronger than it was before.

It's funny that we often recognize people by their flaws. The gap, the dimples, the mole, the scars, the glasses, the accent, the limp. With a perfected mask on we aren't quite sure if we are with a loved one or their doppelgänger. Our stretch marks and scars are recorded history. Maybe my stomach isn't flat and has stretch marks on it, but I have two beautiful sons who lived in there for nine months before being born healthy at almost eight pounds each. My family is full of dimpled cheeks, which is somehow a coveted flaw. The keloids, which are actually sought-after in other parts of the world including the motherland, remind me that the journey didn't kill me, it indeed made me stronger.

Playing dress-up was fun. The last time I did something like this for myself is when I graduated from Suitland High School, many moons ago. It certainly put a bright spot in my day, week, month, and year. We all have not-so-good memories of tough times we spent in quarantine for the COVID-19 Global Pandemic. If that wasn't enough, there was civil unrest and disputed election results threatening to heighten that uneasy feeling of this time. Prophetic voices are predicting everything that I have been scared to read about in Revelation.

But what about the good that has come out of this? In dark times the light shines so much brighter. When I opened Pandora, the next morning, the first song that came on was *Potter's House* by Tremaine Hawkins. I love that song and the massage that the Potter wants to put us back together again. As the Body let's take this time to let our collective light shine, flaws and all.

Verses:

Jeremiah 18:1-4

Isaiah 45:9

Romans 9:19-21

2 Corinthians 12:9

Daniel 10:19

Psalm 139:14

Isaiah 58:8

Challenge:

Let God's light shine through your perceived imperfections. Be light and salt by showing love to Your God, your neighbor and even your enemy, just the way God equipped you to do.

Prayer:

God, thank You for allowing Jasmine Williams, Kenya Rucker and Ms. Didi Green to work together in concert to accentuate what You created. Thank You for allowing me and others to see beauty in what You have fearfully and wonderfully made. My life is now an open book. I love You, Amen!

My Notes

CPSIA information can be obtained
at www.ICGtesting.com
Printed in the USA
BVHW052257070421
604338BV00008B/963